LIST OF ILLUSTRATIONS

CW01506539

Ted Ellis's Countryside Reflections

with 78 drawings by David Poole

Wilson-Poole Publishers
27 Greenborough Road
Sprowston
Norwich NR7 9HQ, Tel 37402

First published September 1982

ISBN 0 9506592 4 X

Phototypeset by Hugh Wilson Typesetting, Norwich
Repro by Photomation, Norwich
Printed and bound in the United Kingdom by Page Bros (Norwich) Ltd.

CONTENTS

ACKNOWLEDGEMENTS

The publisher would like to express his thanks to the following for their helpfulness in the preparation of this publication.

Alan Atherton, librarian Eastern Counties Newspapers, who kindly allowed me access to photographic files in his charge containing photographs of Ted Ellis.

Chris Carter and staff of BBC Television, All Saints Green, Norwich who supplied me with two very valuable stills of Ted taken when he received a television award on the programme, 'Weekend'.

Bridget Yates, curator, Norfolk Rural Life Museum, Gressenhall who supplied me with a selection of the most precious photographs depicting rural life many years ago – two or three of which I selected and drew into the text.

The President and members of Royal Air Force Swanton Morley Officers' Mess for their kind permission to use a drawing (page 40) of the local parish church and three watercolours in their possession (pages 86, 114 and 120).

Denis Whitehead for his warm friendship and tremendous skill in capturing 'glimpses' of Ted in various situations enabling me to draw in more detail the cover, frontispiece, pages 32, 61 and 104, the latter being the Southwold-Walberswick ferryman.

Foreword

Even if caged by circumstances beyond his control into an urban surrounding, the average Englishman is a countryman at heart. This is but one reason why this book from Ted Ellis, long awaited by his admirers, will have an instant appeal to many beyond those whose breakfast reading for the past 36 years has been enhanced by his cherished articles in the *Eastern Daily Press*.

Ted Ellis is renowned however not only as a writer, but as a broadcaster of exceptional talent. Small wonder that for the past decade he has proved one of the most popular contributors to the Regional B.B.C., receiving more letters than anyone else.

On natural history he is an expert without pretension, an observer of remarkable perception and an enthusiast with a keen sense of humour and a generous resolve to share his knowledge with a wide audience of all ages. As a writer he has a style which is refreshingly natural, so that the reader really feels on equal terms with the author and as if he is sharing an experience. The poems give us a glimpse of the romantic.

Above all Ted Ellis is a character in an age when individuality is a scarce commodity. This determination has been to interpret and to share the delights of natural history with his fellow men.

Today many are aware of the mounting pressures on that part of England which deep down we treasure most and call the countryside. What is harder to quantify is the cumulative effect of champions like Ted Ellis in helping to multiply that understanding which in turn generates a desire to actually take part in protecting our natural heritage. I believe it is considerable and I am delighted that this book has been published, not only as a joy to read but to perpetuate an influence which can only be described as admirable.

Bixley Manor   Timothy Colman
Norwich

Author's Note

Having been introduced to this life on an enchanted island where thyme-scented cliffs and rock-pools, butterflies and wheeling gulls evoked delight and curiosity from the very beginning with the ever changing colours and moods of the sea awakening a sense of beauty and wonder at the majesty of Nature in wider view, the days of my childhood were filled with pleasure.

In 1920 the scene changed to one of broader horizons when the family moved to an ancestral base on the Norfolk coast. At first the grey North Sea was a disappointment after the scintillating clarity and rainbow hues of Channel waters, while I missed the grandeur of rocky precipices tufted with thrift and samphire and the fern-banked lanes of my beloved Guernsey. But soon my expeditions along the seashore were providing new thrills, such as the arrival of migrant birds in autumn, while the soft, crumbling cliffs became a fresh source of interest with their revelation of dramatic intrusions by glaciers and the presence of an ancient fossil forest containing remains of extinct animals.

I found enchantment in vast sweeps of marshland criss-crossed with dykes that held curious plants, insects and snails. I made the acquaintance of adders and natterjacks on local heaths and dunes, little red harvest mice in the cornfields and nightjars purring after sundown in shadowy pine woods.

It was not long before I came to enjoy the friendship and help of older naturalists in Great Yarmouth, each imbued with enthusiasm for the special study of birds, plants, insects, microscopic pond life or the treasure of the sea. The doyen of them all was A.H. Patterson, whose young disciple I became. In the years of our companionship he opened up new vistas by introducing me to the mudflats of Breydon and many of his favourite haunts on the Broads. He was the author of numerous books on the natural history of east Norfolk and for very many years his nature notes, illustrated by lively sketches, appearing over his pen-name 'John Knowlittle', delighted readers of the *Eastern Daily Press*. He not only gave me courage to seek a career as a naturalist, but offered succinct advice on putting pen to paper.

In due course I became happily ensconced as a professional naturalist at Norwich Castle Museum and continued in this occupation for twenty-eight years. Much of my spare time was given to participation in the activities of natural history societies and the Norfolk Naturalists' Trust.

Although investigating and recording details of the flora and fauna of East Anglia and other regions have absorbed my attention to a great extent over the years, I have never lost the sense of wonder and delight of adventuring in wild places in all weathers, day and night, season by season. In 1946 the late Mr. Tom Copeman, then editor of the *Eastern Daily Press*, invited me to contribute a daily 'Countryside' note. This happy relationship with a newspaper of fine tradition has continued ever since, allowing me scope for describing and sharing exciting experiences. A selection of these essays, with the occasional poem, occupies the major part of this book. Since 1964 I have also been a regular contributor to the *Guardian's* 'A Country Diary' and some of these offerings have been included.

David Poole's illustrations speak for themselves and I am grateful to him for contributing some of his finest work here. Artists have many ways of portraying what they see and feel and in deft and sympathetic hands the pencil can be a magic tool.

Ted Ellis

Summer Broad

Surlingham, July 1st, 1947

Rain was falling gently and steadily as we set out in the punt for Rockland Broad this evening. The tide was low and the shores of dyke and channel were draped with little tents of pale green algae caught on old stalks and drifted litter. Skirting a bush-grown island we caught glimpses of ripe red currants hanging over the water and hardly touched by birds; the fragrance of guelder rose had given place to the heavy scent of privet blossom and where only a few weeks ago the yellow flags stood in their fullest glory, the poker heads of reed-mace were scattering pollen that came to rest on rain-beads like a faint dust of gold.

Yellow water lilies grew thickest in the shallows where the tides ran most swiftly over beds of shells and stones; many of the spent flowers, their anthers rotting fast into brown jelly, seemed to be getting waterlogged and prostrated, careless of their position and submitting to every drag of the tide. The waters were teeming with fish fry, some of which made sallies at dead moths floating by.

We surprised several family parties of ducks at the bends in the Fen Channel; the mallard included small ducklings and noisy 'flappers,' with a few drakes in their brown eclipse plumage. Despite the presence of so many marauding crows in the nesting season, our mallard, teal and shoveller have increased tremendously this year, judging by the numbers we saw at Rockland; they were bobbing about on the waters everywhere, with grebes and their young, while spectral herons looked on from every vantage point that could be filled.

Dewpoint Flashes

Surlingham, August 13th, 1947

I went out on the marshes just after dawn, at the moment when the sun had begun to conjure forth a blurred brightness from the veil of night and to break the spell of the mist brooding like a ghostly snowdrift upon the fen. Then a million twinkling lights appeared on reed and grass and gossamer everywhere. Not a leaf or flower seemed to be without its magic spider, its geometrician and spinner of silken cradles. What a night it must have been; the spiders must have found in the dew and the breathless calm all the delight and promise of a glorious day to come. As I stood still and felt the first warmth of the sun upon my face I realised that an owl was doing exactly the same on an oak bough stretched across the dyke beside me.

Arripo and the Dawn Fairy

'It's my birthday', thought Arripo, waking in the starlight and wondering if he should go to sleep again. 'Yes, it is your birthday, dear Arripo,' whispered the Dawn Fairy, dancing in through the open window at that moment with the smallest and most beautiful lantern imaginable swinging from her hand, 'and if you wish, you may get up at once, take my rose-light and go wake the rest of the world for me. This is my birthday too, Arripo, and I'd like to spend it tucked away in your little bed. I've seen all the world many times. I'm sure you'd like to take my place for once, wouldn't you?'

Arripo was only five years old that morning and he knew no more about the world than that it was a place people talked about. He'd heard of people going to the ends of it, out into it and around it. So he thought it would be very nice to take the little lamp; then he could have a really good look at the world before he woke it up, perhaps: but where should he find it?

'Oh, you don't have to find it,' explained the fairy, 'because it's here, there and everywhere. Now it's time to be off. Come with me. All you have to do is to sit astride the first sunbeam we meet and it'll carry you right round the world and home again.'

Then Arripo held the fairy's hand while she whisked him away into the starry sky. They were only just in time. The first sunbeam arrived exactly as their rose-lantern threw a magical blush over a wisp of cloud above them. And as the glistening world began to wake, Arripo set out on his journey while the fairy slipped away to take her rest.

Birds greeted his passing with songs from the tree-tops and in the sky itself. Great clouds and snowy mountains seemed to catch fire before him. He saw the rose-light dance on the waves of the sea and flash upon all pools and windows. Even the ugly smoke of cities was changed into a curtain shimmering between earth and heaven.

So Arripo spent his birthday, filled with the greatest happiness he had ever known. The time passed quickly and he was surprised when the Dawn Fairy flew up to meet him—so surprised that he dropped the lantern, right over his own house. 'Never mind,' said the fairy. 'Look, the Wings of the Morning have caught it—away they go. They'll look after it now. You see I've been carrying it around for years and years and now I'm going to have a change. The Fairy Queen has granted me a special wish. I've decided to become a little sister for you, Arripo. go to sleep now and I shall be your birthday present when you wake next time. Keep our secret, won't you?'

Low over Water

Surlingham, August 25th, 1947

A blur of thin cloud hid the moon as we crept out upon the waters tonight, but the sky was luminous enough to throw the waterside alders and sallows into sharp relief and to accentuate the blackness of their shadows. Patches of duckweed drifting on the tide seemed much thicker somehow than by day and looked like solid islands built of sand; one almost expected to see Lilliputian ships sailing into their little harbours.

When my spell of quanting was over I lay full length peering forward over the bows of the punt and enjoying as near as possible a water-vole's view of the world. The fringing reeds then seemed to spear the very sky; they might have been tall Papyrus beside the Nile and their feathery tops disappeared in a sort of airy freckling towards the clouds. The upturned edge of a water-lily leaf took on the appearance of a great black obstacle and when a frightened moorhen flopped out of a bush and landed in the water, it seemed to set up as great a commotion as a whale might have done.

I had never realised before that things would look so different when seen from the actual surface of a dyke.

Fish Frolic

Surlingham, September 30th, 1947

Tonight we had a rather exciting experience on the pool called 'Deep Waters,' but which is no longer deep. The tide was racing out and our punt emerged from Broad Dyke with a swirl as though it had just shot the rapids of a highland stream. Then, as we were borne more gently across the broad the full moon appeared over the top of a cloud bank in the east, and from that moment, when the waters became flecked with liquid gold, we became aware of a sudden agitation all about us. While we floated silently on the tide fishes leapt out of the water in high frolic on every side and away as far as we could see; in the bright pathway of the moon's reflection scores of little fishes thrust their noses above the surface and swam about so fast that they might almost have been packs of miniature sharks cleaving the air with top-sail fins. They may have been young bream stirring up the mud for a nocturnal fest, but I am more inclined to think they were roach feeling a little giddy in the moonbeams, for we have seen great numbers of these fishes here lately—almost as many as at spawning time in May.

A Winter's End

In early March Rockland Broad was still so ice-bound that boats could not creep out upon it from the regular staithe; but a friend and I were able to reach an expanse of open water to the east where tides still swept in from the river and streamed by way of the Fen Channel northwards through the Surlingham marshes. We disturbed cormorants at their fishing and startled an ungainly goosander. Hundreds of coot walked away slowly across the ice, like an army of black pygmies. Whooper swans rose from the ice-flat, trumpeting majestically. Flocks of tufted duck shone black and white in the sunshine as they encircled us, flying with great bunches of pochard, mallard, teal and wigeon. The sound of rushing wings filled the air, combining with the music of lapping water as it threshed the ice and honeycombed its margin with little craters curiously like those upon the dead moon. Away to the west a cloud of perhaps three thousand black-headed gulls rose noisily in a dark funnel-shaped mass resembling more than anything a waterspout at sea. They were still there when we stole out upon the water by moonlight that evening, having settled in a dense mass on the ice. On the night of 5 March, in a snowstorm which for all its smothering failed to obscure the radiance of a nearly full moon, we pressed our narrow duck-punt into service against a nor'-easter and a boiling tide and presently approached the gull-roost. The birds were huddled as a dark pack on the ice near the centre of the broad; not one rested on the water of the shining 'wake' through which we made our passage. Presently they rose sullenly like smoke from a smouldering volcano and whirled about us in utter silence; we found it an eerie experience, as though the shadows of a spirit world had closed in upon us. Moments later they began to settle and as we slipped away we saw that they had created once more the dusky island which had dissolved so strangely at our coming.

On the night of 16th March a great gale roared through the woods and hissed upon the marshes, carrying with it a stinging hail of twigs and reed-stuff. Just before the wind rose it became apparent that something unusual was astir, for birds were in a state of excitement as they gathered at their roosts. Grey clouds scudded faster and faster across the sky, and presently the gulls which had assembled on the broad decided to leave in a body, screaming as they beat their way westwards to settle on a field for the night.

Moonplay

This evening, as a bright crescent moon was dipping towards the west, we set out in the punt to savour the magic of an autumn night upon the waters. Soon, familiar landmarks seemed to have receded and become dissolved into smudges, wisps and curtains of pale tracery. Reed beds and their reflections took on a peculiar squareness and from the water line at a little distance they loomed out of the black setting of the carrs beyond like the hulks of Spanish galleons or graceful longships beset with oars. Moonbeams shone on the wave-crests of grass in the swamps and transformed the freckles and streaks of waterweeds into a semblance of newly-formed ice, while drops of water hanging on leaves scintillated like diamonds as we drifted past. The darkness and the silvering, the small white clouds like distant snow-caps glimpsed above the black brush tops of sallow bushes, and pale snakines of boughs dipping in the water, the night's canopy of dusky blue—there came a moment when we shuddered in this chill dreamland—the dreamland, surely, of John Sell Cotman.

Fulfilment

Deep in the pool of life all wonders sleep.
   Yet at a touch are summoned to disport,
Full-sensed and yielding gaily to the will
   That lures them from the silence and the gloom.

Like winking bubbles in a glass they rise,
   All iridescent, leaping to be free
And every moment changing their design:
   A destiny in every random gleam.

So butterflies are born to brave the air,
   As pastel poplars grace the flowing breeze;
As dolphins arc and dive in ecstasy
   And children run upon the sands in glee.

But for the burning genius of the sun,
   The pale moon's Cupid glance upon the earth
And every rhythm pulsed from farther space,
   Creation's sweet fulfilment had not come.

When memory's eye looks down the aisles of Time,
   Let golden dreams dissolve the mists of grief;
Then, in the shadow and the light, the years
   Will wake and pass in beauty, one by one.

Like daffodils the young friends dance again;
   Love's roses linger in the summer dusk;
Glowing the harvest where ripe wisdom dwells
   And innocent December's quiet farewell.

(1977)

The Snipe Marsh

Surlingham, January 8th, 1948

This afternoon I walked over to a little snipe marsh where the flowering bogbean sparkles and cotton-grass shakes out white billows of fluff in spring and where through the summer broad ribbons of various rushes and sedges weave a rich pattern in every shade of living green. Today, in winter's fitful sunshine, the place looked desolate indeed—a brown and tousled waste, dark-pooled with flood waters, a sunken and dejected hinterland serving as a mere fore-stage foil to the shining reed-beds beyond.

But when I waded into the bog (with care) and took a closer look at the vegetation, it became suddenly intricate and beautiful. The whorled branchlets of marsh horsetail were spread about like embroideries of silver hair. Flag leaves, grey speckled with moulds, lay in limp snaky tangles. The cotton grass formed soft red-brown tussocks through which could be seen their still living dark green leaf-bases. Where last summer's rushes lay quite flat, new green spikes had grown through the mat like needles; and many a small green leaf was making the most of the winter daylight while taller competitors were laid low awhile.

Stirrings in the Frost

10th January, 1948

There is only a delicate lacing of snow on the fields here, forming rippled patterns caused by the interplay of sun and wind; but the ground is rock-hard, even along woodland glades, with sub-zero temperatures persisting day and night. Even so, moles are still breaking through the crust and I prodded soft earth newly pushed to the surface this afternoon. Still pools are frozen firmly everywhere and now, swept by an icy blast from the East, even the tidal waters are fighting a losing battle with the frost and wildfowl are to be seen congregating on rafts of ice where only yesterday they were swimming freely.

Except for the faint moaning of the wind and the cries of excited gulls here and there, a chill silence prevails, in the glare of winter's sunshine. Looking across the marshes this afternoon, without a bird in view, I found most pleasure in watching the reed plumes, softly beating the air like wings of doves in their golden setting.

Low Tide on the Broad

Surlingham, January 11th, 1948

With a new moon this morning we expected a spring tide; instead a southerly gale held back the oncoming flood in the North Sea, and as a result we experienced a continuous ebb in the Yare waters for twelve hours on end. Mudflats became exposed in the Broads round about mid-day, and by 8 p.m. the water had reached the lowest level we have ever known here. Rockland Broad came to look like Breydon, with high shelf-like mud banks intersected by branching channels.

In places water-lilies sprouting from the mud appeared to be growing on dry land and reeds round the shores stood in towering clumps, with three feet of stalk exposed below the usual cutting level, and with encrustations of sponges patching their blackened slimy bases. Empty valves of freshwater mussels littered the mud, and as the white shell beds emerged in the Fen Channel air got into thousands of little shells, causing them to float away.

We took the punt down as far as Rockland Fleet during the evening and found navigation quite a tricky business, what with shoals, jagged remains of water-borne trees and sunken wrecks. For a time we lay under the shelter of the hulk of a sunken wherry, her stern, complete with rudder, high and dry; the old boat seemed to have come to life again after having lain hidden under a thick blanket of mud, reeds and sallow bushes for many years. The birds we noticed seemed slightly awed and nervous—acutely aware of a strangeness in their surroundings. In the lantern light a moorhen fluttered as light as a moth and dropped straight into my lap in the boat, while a huge coypu skulked stolidly on the shore, eyeing us with interest.

A Glance at Sunset

Surlingham, February 4th, 1948

Even pranky schoolboys on the bus were silent as they stole glances at the coral sunset on their way homeward yesterday. Perhaps the vertical pillar of light, shooting into the heavens like the beam of an aurora, impressed them as it parted the ripples of fire. Like the strangely silent rooks and daws flapping away to their roosting places, they must have felt that some magic was afoot. And this morning the sky was clear at dawn, so that quite soon the whole countryside became clothed in a soft radiance. Farmsteads and cottages stood forth like the turrets of fairyland, picked out in white, buttercup or darkling red. Every one of ten thousand trees was defined with grace and individual majesty. Straw in the stackyards gleamed like the sun itself and the fields were so transfigured that they no longer seemed to belong to our rural workaday world, but to be part of the architecture of dreams and of the peace that passeth all understanding.

Patchwork Day

Surlingham, February 19th, 1948

This has been a patchwork day of snow squalls and sunshine. As I came down the lane this afternoon I could actually sniff the sweetness of blossoming gorse along its banks; yet the hills of Strumpshaw across the valley lay white under winter's spell and looking westward over the nearest field I was almost blinded by the violet-blue dappling of snow, like dancing water, that bewitched the furrowed soil. Presently, in the woods, I saw polished scarlet ladybirds clustering about bare twigs and a yellow brimstone butterfly still torpid in the cleft of a gale-cracked tree. Then came a whirling of the snow and leaden clouds smothered the sun's last defiant flare of orange in the west.

In early evening the sky cleared and a half moon and the evening star glittered upon the white-flecked scene, so we were tempted forth upon the water. A white and rather ghostly punt nosed its way along dark, tortuous channels and across the grey, slapping waters of the Broads. Waterhens tumbled out of bushes, teal whistled in the shadows, mallard rose with noisy protestations. A heron startled us with a loud 'frank!' as he flapped from a sheltered bay; soaring, he met a baffling gust and came swooping down again across our bows—a huge, black scarecrow. Returning, a hailstorm overtook us and for some minutes the reed-beds all about us crackled like tinfoil; then fine snow came in the wake of the hail and seemed to quiver above the fen like the will-o'-the-wisp mist of a summer's night.

Evening Calm

Surlingham, March 16th, 1948

In a perfect calm this evening we crept out into the middle of Rockland Broad and lay there in our punt while the shades of night descended. No sunset gold even momentarily lightened the greyness of sky. The broad—a seemingly vast expanse of water—gleamed like softly polished pewter, its surface unbroken by so much as a bubble. No mist hung in the valley, yet as the light faded every bush and shadow round the shore became smudged and unsubstantial—bewitched into something as delicate as a watery jotting in an artist's sketch-book.

Pale bands of reed narrowed to vanishing point; the water became blotchy with the shades of night clouds; the silhouettes hardened. For an hour the air was full of harsh and musical sounds. Snipe drummed, redshanks piped, grebe growled, garganey rattled, wood owls hooted, barn owls screeched, teal whistled, water-hens bubbled, herons uttered raucous cries and coot made water music as they rushed about in play. Then the night became colder and as we glided out of the shadow of Tom's Hole and passed by the black skeleton willow which marks the site of Kruger's Island, there remained no trace of soft, grey evening: a brittle and unkindly atmosphere bid us begone and every living creature of a sudden became silent.

The Peewits

Surlingham, April 14th, 1948

This evening we paid a visit to the peewits' nesting ground. Here was no stony upland field such as many of these birds delight in, but a sodden meadow full of holes and hillocks made by horses grazing year after year over the soft peaty land. What grass existed there was wire-fine and cropped to the smoothness of a lawn; its new growth gleamed bice green with the slanting light of sunset upon it; hundreds of little knolls were silhouetted brightly against a vast low carpet of moss, picked out here and there with king-cups and sedge-leaves bleached almost to silver.

The peewits had scraped shallow depressions in the hummocks, some by way of experiment, others in earnest, and dotted about we found their eggs in clusters of four. These varied in their dark blotching and ground tint, but all were some shade of olive-fawn, easily escaping notice in the midst of so many vegetable greens and browns. On one mound larger than most others a snipe had laid her glossy eggs and made sure that they were partly hidden by a wisp of rushes. Oddly enough, there was no sign of the birds until we were about to leave; the evening was warm and the eggs had not been brooded long, so the birds were not worrying for their safety.

Journey at Twilight

Surlingham, May 28th, 1948

Punting homeward from Rockland Staithe late this evening I drew into the shade of a willow tree and enjoyed for a few moments the utter peace of Broadland. The waters seemed to have a frozen stillness and with the discs and upturned edges of lily leaves, the spiky blackness of the reeds at dusk, the silhouettes of herons and great noctule bats against the sky and the pure silver of the great expanse of Broad, I was reminded of the prettiest artistry of Japan—the flashing metalwork of storks and dragons, willow trees and laughing water and the black lacquer of their embedding.

Presently I stole forward again, with the reflection of a rose-cream cloud gliding ahead as the moon sails in the sky, thence into the narrower channel, passing yellow flags staring like fixed stars out of the twilight and galaxies of blossoms clustered about the guelder rose branches low over the water, until I came to the Home Staithe and heard the babble of the little waterfall that gushes from the sluice as the tide runs outs.

Haven of Terns

Blakeney Point, June 3rd, 1948

The tide was up and a stiff breeze from westward hissed over the water, so that we enjoyed a frolicsome and somewhat spumy voyage from Morston Quay to the Point this afternoon. Dark rain squalls swept across the sky and the long lines of dunes, with their clean, bleached hummocks of sand, the brightness of distant creeks and the crinkled, glistening mudbanks of the saltings near at hand together formed a grey and silver scene more in keeping with a mood of winter than in the nature of a fleeting crossness in the the face of June.

Landing on a spit near the old lifeboat house, we followed the curve of a shingle ridge fringed raggedly with *Suaeda* bushes, where white sea campion blossomed between the stones and rose pink cushions of thrift lent colour to the drift lines strewn with rubbish and thousands of small bleaching crab shells. Rain had refreshed the vegetation of the desert sandhills and between chalk green tufts of marram a starry moss (*Tortula*) had expanded in rich carpets which, in the peculiar light, appeared more golden than mossy.

Presently, towards the margin of the sea, where the marrams were more scant, and blue, sand-splashed flints of larger size lay scattered, we met the terns, the pearl-grey sea-swallows, and were chided by them as we stole looks at their eggs cupped amongst the pebbles. The birds had been sitting while the squall lasted and had left their wedge-shaped silhouettes patterned in dry sand.

Weird Twilight

Surlingham, June 14th, 1948

An almost tropical day has ended in a weird twilight. The evening has been one of breathless calm, with a haze risen high to dim the twinkling light and hold the atmosphere below in bondage. At Yarmouth I could not see the faintest rim of horizon betwixt sea and sky. Passing Breydon, I looked on wet mud flats and ribboning channels and saw them as an embroidery of softest silk. Under the shrouded sky the grazing marshes became green as an Irish bog, then brighter and brighter with thick sprinklings of buttercups as I came up the valley of the Yare. By the time I reached Brundall and Coldham Hall the sunset glow was tingeing millions of blobs of cuckoo-spit on the willows and wayside herbage with the pinkness of strawberry ice, and as I walked home by the lanes the sweet heavy fragrance of white campion blossom and honeysuckle filled the air. Now, at half-past ten, as I take a last turn round the garden, moths are rising from the grass and trees and vanishing into the twilight, and huge black slugs are stealing forth, already wet with dew; but the valley is filled with silence—not even an owl has broken the spell in the past half hour. The gloaming has become the dead of night uncannily soon.

Foam and Sand-drift

Scolt Head Island, July 5th, 1948

Yesterday evening the last ragged fringes of the rain curtain vanished and for a moment the sun appeared to glorify the sea with a trail of fire. Then came an ominous calm below, while three distinct layers of clouds were agitated by criss-cross currents in the heavens. The wind shifted to the north-west and freshened quickly to a gale, which smote us furiously all through the grey night. This morning the white horses were flying towards the beach and great walls of foam were quivering and spilling over the tidemark. Much of the foam, concentrated to a sort of half-melted sticky essence as its iridescent bubbles subsided, became resolved into grey-brown scum, revealing the presence of fine mud carried hither from the Wash, as well as bilge oil and other less tangible flotsam. When the wind freed lumps of this stuff they went bowling along, picking up an increasing crust of mud and beach sand until the accumulation of an extreme load proved their undoing; their progress was marked by groove-like tracks, so that the beach came to look as though it had been combed with a rake.

Tons of sand were being swept from the shore into the shelter of the marram hills. The finer particles made a blizzard mist whisked high into the air, while larger grit and fragments of shells could be seen trickling up slopes and shuffling round obstructions like grain being jiffled out of a threshing machine. The sharp flinty leaves of the marram grass went into action in a curious way; as the wind blew off and on they cut semi-circular grooves in the sand so that the hillocks on which they grew became fortified with a series of holls and ditches, like ancient earthworks.

Butterfly Fen

Surlingham, August 1st, 1948

The fen is now one bright ribbon of flowers and dancing butterflies. Almost overcome by the shimmering heat this morning, I waded a little way through a sea of tall brown-knotted rushes and foamy drifts of meadowsweet to watch the glorious peacocks and tortoise-shells imbibing sweetness from their favourite blossoms. They came to the old rose tassels of hemp agrimony, to the delicate pink spires of marsh woundwort, to the magenta purple loosestrife, the button heads of knapweed and nectarous marsh thistles. Other flowers, filling niches with a spread of gold, white and blue, appeared to hold no charm for butterflies.

The tufted vetch, massed in great crests of hyacinth blue and amethyst, received no visitors but certain little bumble-bees. The meadowsweet and white tresses of bog bedstraw attracted yellow and black-striped hover flies, which stole their pollen. Other flowers, for all their loveliness to the sight by day, would hold themselves to keep tryst with the pale moths at dusks and dawn, or even to supply the needs of sweet-loving male mosquitoes while the females went in quest of blood.

Thorn on the Heath

The thorn is dark up on the heath
  This winter day
And the hill is crowned with a red fern wreath,
  Raggedly gay.
The sun is silvered in a cloud;
  The wind is chill
And woods are wrapt in a sea-mist cloud
  By Weybourne Mill.
The birch trees gleam in dancing light
  Beyond the dell
Where they will stand like ghosts tonight,
  Witching a spell:
A spell of beauty and of life
  In mist and dark.
Yet the bent thorn's beauty, born of strife,
  Is for the lark
That knows the freedom of the air
  And nightly dies.
So, when I look upon the fair
  And face the wise,
The uplift' heart of the lark in me
  Soars for the brave.
'Tis the crooked thorn I look to see:
  Not the white witch-stave.

(1949)

Stirrings in Trees

Surlingham, September 29th, 1948

Tonight as I stood at the gate, content with the peace of a starry sky and moved by the beauty of a solitary elm tree silhouetted against the lingering afterglow in the west, I found myself listening to the progress of a succession of little swirling gusts of air through the tree-tops in the wood away on my left. The elm kept silence; the fluttering of its leaves was as the trembling of ribbon weeds in a stream; but the oaks were stirred at times to something like sabre-rattling and their billowy crests never ceased from the crisp rustling that one associates with silks and satins.

I walked over to a giant beech only to find that its half-bare twigs were free from the gossip of jostling leaves. The aspens whispered in what I would describe as silvery whispers. The nut trees had spread their leaves so primly and methodically that nothing less than a hurricane would have moved them to make an audible swish. A thin pattering like the momentary sprinkling of raindrops from the edge of a cloud was all that the breeze could evoke from the ashes, and the pines, though their dark needle-nested boughs might rock like cradles, tonight at least produced no whisper of a lullaby.

Rainbow Weather

Surlingham, November 8th, 1948

We have experienced a fair measure of what might be termed 'rainbow weather' recently and many a splendid arc has spanned the sky between brightness and shower. Displays of prismatic colours were especially frequent today, and many a worker in the fields must have rejoiced in the added touch of beauty to the sweep of autumn's sparkling landscape, with its frescoes of half-golden trees, its trails of fiercely crimsoned berries, its voyaging cloud shadows, shining corn ricks, purple hollows in the ploughlands and its gleaming snow-white gulls settling everywhere like so many hungry infant angels.

When night came the moon shone forth fitfully as the sun had coursed through the day, and while the breeze died away from the land and frost was soon crisping the grass, great clouds sped by in the upper air and now and again dipped low enough to startle the sleeping valley with a dark squall. During one such episode we were bringing a boat home along the Fen Channel and as the rain curtain approached from the north-east we saw the white arc of a lunar rainbow vaulting its darkness. There was a full bow, but only half a moon to make it; that doesn't seem to matter!

Journey Through Fog

Surlingham, November 23rd, 1948

The fog which has brooded over the land like a plague of Egypt for the past two days still clung with ghostly stillness about us tonight. Moisture dripped from the trees in chilled droplets, breaking the silence but drearily, and owls went about hooting and screeching as though they might have come to the end of their patience with the fog's obstructionism.

For the adventure of it we made a journey by punt through a maze of channels and pools and across the broad to Rockland Staithe. There was a faint glimmer of light upon the water despite the thick darkness of the night, and we just managed to find our way, guided by our recognition of little promontories looming out of the haze here and there. However vigorously we paddled, the boat seemed to make little or no progress, because we could not see the banks flashing by; it was like the frustration of a treadmill.

Ill-defined blotches and walls of darkness warned us of the presence of the taller reed beds and trees; they seemed to lie several yards away when we were actually nosing into them, and at one point a fallen willow's branches seemed to reach out of the mist and grapple with us in our blindness. We were surprised to hear the familiar shuffling of starlings still roosting in the wet and dreary reeds and wondered how they had managed to find their way to such a sleeping place wrapped in autumn's thickest and chilliest fog.

A Frosted World

Surlingham, November 29th, 1948

The frozen fog has collected in little particles on every twig and leaf and built a sparkling fairyland beneath the cloak of general gloom. Tonight I held a lamp aloft as I went down a loke to the marshes and followed a winding path through the woods so that I should see details of the shimmering spectacle. Oak leaves, weighted with thick frills of ice along their margins, kept tinkling down from the tree-tops, and where they landed on a hard surface the ice upon them whizzed into the air again in dust-like splinters, like blizzard powder scattered by descending snowballs. I noticed that all thorns and prickles on brambles, wild roses, gorse bushes and the like had become square-tipped with white crystals.

Hedgerow bushes were hung with shining stalactites and festooned with crystal rods, loops and bridges of encrusted gossamer, Hawthorn berries seemed to be trimmed with ermine, and many of them were adorned with five-pointed silver stars. Orb-webs of spiders had been transformed into snares of chain-mail. Holly leaves were all edged with silver, while the waxen leaves of laurel and rhododendron were stiff with thin, faintly-rippled ice. Nodding thistle-heads had assumed the form of snow-sprinkled pine cones. Even the barbed wire had lost its terrors in frozen tresses of gossamer.

A Walk in the Rain

North Norfolk, January 3rd, 1950

This afternoon I walked to a little copse straggling down to the brink of a disused gravel pit. Rain fell steadily and brought out the fragrance of dead leaves, mosses, fungi lurking under the trees, the aromatic wood sage omni-present on the hedge-banks, and the sweet clover hay being trundled along the road just then in a farm waggon.

I stood for a moment drinking in the beauty of a tuft of yellow gorse glimpsed beyond a wilderness of arched bramble stems, which shone with a crimson glory of their own where they footed the grey winter sky. Here and there a rose hip glowed like a beacon amongst the bushes, appearing the more brilliant owing to the complete lack of berries on the hawthorns massed above them.

Then a thrush broke into song, perched low on a sapling oak, and as his silvery challenge rang out I forgot the winter and the rain. But soon the purring of a tractor away on the stony ploughland broke the spell, and as I turned to retrace my steps I became only too conscious of the dim curtain that shall hide the spring for three months more.

April Storm

Surlingham, April 2nd, 1950

We watched the progress of a brief storm across the marshes this afternoon. For a while the reed beds gleamed whitely where shafts of sunlight smote them through rifts in the forward, curling clouds, and the alder trees looked almost fiery in the warmth of their colouring against the darkness of the lowering heavens beyond.

Then came the chill onslaught of rain, and at the first thunder-clap wood doves came hurtling over our heads as their terror of the storm impelled them to seek refuge out of its path.

A wetting yellowed the ribbon leaves of the sedges and darkened to a rosy orange tint the stiff little catkins and the bog myrtle bushes. Presently the blue sky opened in the west, with high white clouds enamelled upon it. As the darkness fled the fen became a paradise, for the sallows became pricked out in silver and gold of catkins, the occasional birches took on

a dazzling brightness as though illumined by the lightning itself, and the golden osiers glistened like the petals of buttercups.

Two very black crows came forth to forage, like the first of their tribe to wander over the face of the earth after Noah's flood. Then a wren whirred on to the top of a bush and sang a ditty of rejoicing; the storm was over.

Aurora Borealis

Surlingham, January 25th, 1949

From the edge of the fen, where a thin mantle of frost-laden mist stretched before me like the chill face of the polar ice-cap itself, I saw the star-pricked sky tonight most gloriously disturbed. Aurora borealis is shy and fickle in appearing here and I suppose we must never expect a display to match in jewelled brightness that arc of flames and rainbow streamers which as children we were led to believe illuminated long winter nights in the land of Santa Claus.

Nevertheless, what I saw of the shifting radiance of the Northern Lights tonight was magical enough. From the Great Bear to the Seven Sisters and spurting far beyond the zenith at times, shafts and broken ribbons of pale electric green and soft effulgences of crimson mist, exactly the colour of a bullfinch's breast, glowed and were gone, reappearing in the twinkling of an eye with all the fitfulness of a will-o'-the wisp.

I found it most difficult to focus on any one area of the heavens long enough to see the rhythm of dancing particles, but what else could one expect of electrified motes swirling into the earth's high atmosphere with fearful speed from the sun?

Wild Weather

Surlingham, February 8th, 1949

There were flurries of white water on the broad tonight as the breeze freshened. Gulls crowded in one of the more sheltered bays were restless and noisy. The quavering notes of a brown owl issued from Surlingham Wood like the wild skirling of bagpipes heard fitfully between the wind gusts. The moon above was encircled by a white ring of misted light at a distance which allowed for the twinkling of many stars between orb and halo—the 'far barrow' ominous of worsening weather. We found ourselves listening more intently than usual to the music of wind and water, to the slapping and tinkling of ripples against the boat, the fret of sallow branchlets against sere reed stems and, whenever we nosed inshore, the catapult thrumming of stubble tips underwater, plucked like bass strings by the punt's bottom in passing.

We glided past beds of leaning 'pokers,' their bleached and broken ribbon leaves gleaming more brightly because of their glancing angularity than the almost vaporous wisps of straight upstanding reed. Moorhens croaked resentfully as we moved up the Fen Channel, while rushing wings and the harsh complaints of female teal and deep voiced mallard smote the mid air. The black shapes of ivy-covered ash and alder trees loomed weirdly from the carrs and one of them we had the whim to liken to that friendly image, the black-leaded, old-time door-stopper, cast-iron Punch.

Paul Klee, Surrealist

*(Impressions gathered at an exhibition of his works
at Norwich in 1946 E.A. Ellis)*

No miniature, no cameo,
   But only quite abstract neo-
Shall satisfy electric mind
   And free the sentimental blind:
So writes Paul Klee upon the wall
   In cryptic patterns, to appal
A smug and straight-laced multitude
   (Or bid one share his solitude).
Like Alice through a Looking Glass
   He must have slipped and stayed to pass
An age of time; yet sending back
   A mystic message through the crack.
But then he smashed the Glass and strode
   Far down the Universal road,
Trading his other-worldly wares
   For nothing more than strangers' stares.
This artist (is he very wrong?)
   Can beckon sunsets all day long.
The curtain of his squinting eye,
   Quivering, mocks a radiant sky,
Peopling sunbeams with strange wings:
   Motes and stars and fairy things.
Imagination sets the stage
   For fitful play in Vision's cage.
A surrealist must dream all day,
   Absorbing here and there a ray
Of Truth that will not be denied
   Its say in curbing Mischief's pride.
Like ripples on the open sea
   His whims and fancies wander free,
Careless of whether you or I
   Would rather stay a little shy.
Perfection's hazed in a twilight land
   Where ghosts dance on the shifting sand
When magic insight points the way
   Beyond the rainbow and the day.
Curious Klee on invisible wire
   Climbs to a perch away from fire
And like a cunning spider spins
   His phantom tracery, and grins!

Kingfishers

Surlingham, April 3rd, 1950

Since my recent mention of a kingfishers's neatly controlled flight within the confines of a room, several correspondents have been kind enough to send me notes about the behaviour of these beautiful birds. Mr. C. E. Brock has had kingfishers in the neighbourhood of Keswick Mill, on the Yare, for the past forty years without a break and on two occasions he remembers birds flying indoors..

Once he noticed a kingfisher trying to get out of his bedroom window, which it had entered previously, through a two-inch opening at the top. More recently he discovered one flying about the ground-floor chamber of the mill and made haste to open the door lest the resident cat should come on the scene, but before he could do this, the bird had returned to the open air through a hole about the size of a human fist in one of the windows.

Mr. Brock often has the pleasure of watching the birds at their fishing as he peers through the mill windows. They hover like kestrels, then dive suddenly upon the small fish in the river, after which they fly off to a perch and consume the silvery catch.

Sudden Winter

Surlingham, April 25th, 1950

Showers of sleet swept hissing upon the reeds this morning and formed a granulated icy crust upon the flood waters of the night tide, which had brimmed over the marshes and now filled every hollow. Under the shadow of sudden winter, birds preserved silence and hid themselves from the fury of the north wind. I thought of shivering swallows, sulking cuckoos and hushed nightingales and of the tiny mites of willow warblers that had poured forth sweet music from high branches everywhere, while the sun twinkled upon a million dancing buds newly leafed but two mornings ago.

Now the tender leaves themselves were being whipped from the trees and bushes and lay like sprigs of icing, so crisply mingled were they with the drifts of small, powdery hail prettily come to rest by stealth on April soil and April grass. While bruised daffodils looked quite forlorn in their prostration before the torturing gusts. I found that not all flowers were at the wind's mercy, for when I went down to see to the safety or our boats I saw that huge clumps of king-cups lay submerged and at peace, blossoming like small golden lilies beneath flood waters.

Stormy Sunset

Surlingham, July 9th, 1950

The air became charged with the vapours of a heat haze today and hour by hour the light played strange tricks over land and sea, until there came the most fantastic and fiercely glorious sunset that we have seen for many a year. During the afternoon I happened to be looking northward along a stretch of shingle beach on the Suffolk coast when I noticed that betwixt the blue level sea and the distant cliff-line a hazy pillar of white light bemused the horizon immediately above the quivering, silvery waves of vapour rising from the shingle bank. Only the rare genius of Cotman or a Turner might have fixed a little vision of this radiance in a seascape for us; how greatly stirred they would have been by such a pure brightness in the heavens!

The sunset I saw from the Yare Valley. First there was a rosy blossoming of clouds in the south-east then a spattering, wisping and un-curling of gold and fiery cloudlets overhead and finally an angry triumph of lightning and thunder as storm messengers swept towards the burning edge of the world. Few who experienced this strange on-coming of a fearful night will forget the defiance of the sun's going down and the ragged omens of the storm.

Summer Evening

Surlingham, July 14th, 1950

As I look out of my window this evening the mellow gold of late sunshine streaks the grass softly and filters between the trees of the oak wood across the way. A white admiral butterfly toys with the high-climbing honeysuckle; a dappled, illusive creature of fairyland. From an oak on the sunny side a solitary thrush is pouring forth a surprisingly sweet little song and a ring dove coos contentedly in an ivy bower.

But silence reigns among the crowds of chaffinches; the shrill wrens and plaintive robins are dumb. Even the nightingale is a changeling now, uttering only harsh curses and warning spitfire cracks of sound from the bushes when he is disturbed. All those silvery whisperings and tremulous voices of the small warblers are missing now. The grasshoppers make dry jiffling sounds underfoot instead; and the solemn zooming of a hornet becomes majestic music in the woods.

When night falls I know that no mewing of owls will break the spell and I shall hear only that faint singing of my own pulses when I stand under the starlit sky and try to imagine, like the ancients, that it is the music of the spheres that floats down through the silence.

An Old Friend

Surlingham, October 12th, 1950

From a hilltop on the North Norfolk coast this afternoon I looked out towards a hazed grey line of sea and all that lonely stretch of dunes and saltings lying between Brancaster and Holkham of the darkling woods. Away over the big creek the marram-tufted bluffs and ridges of Scolt Head Island were visible only as a yellow-brown dappled and scarcely definable smudge with the little observation hut almost merged into the general drabness of the landscape.

In the stillness of shadowy autumn it was not easy to recall earlier memories of that wild and beautiful realm of sea birds and flowers, of pied oyster-catchers piping on shingle, of terns wheeling in a blue sky in their screaming thousands, of foam blowing across the great beds of sea lavender, of baby seals dozing on the beach, of shelduck marching across the green samphire flats.

But I had cause to remember these glories especially today, for in a little while I was to bid farewell to an old friend in whose gallant company I had tramped the island in fair weather and foul through all the years of our acquaintance. Mr. Charles Chestney, was to relinquish his wardenship of the sanctuary. I feel that I must pay tribute to the selfless enthusiasm with which he has carried out his work for the National Trust through the years, and to the kindly help he has given to all naturalists, young and old, whenever they have come to share the delights of his kingdom by the sea.

Signs of Spring

Surlingham, February 25th, 1951

This afternoon we voyaged by punt through a maze of twisting waterways in the sallow carrs and emerged from time to time upon sunlit pools and broads. Winter in the valley still held general sway, yet there were signs of awakening spring enough to encourage the idea that the pulse of life would soon be quickened everywhere. The silver-grey of lichen tufts on the bushes was not relieved by a single green shoot, but on sallow twigs silken buds were swelling and the alders were hung with crimson catkins. Waxwings swooped upon the guelder rose berries and went up to perch again in the leafless ash trees while ringdoves sunned themselves on ivy boughs. Mallard rose in pairs from the bush-grown swamps at every turn and it was clear that they would shortly be nesting.

The great crested grebes had in parts returned from the coast to their breeding quarters in the Broads, while dabchicks from up-river still lingered in those same waters which they had sought in winter. We saw no patches of green blanket weeds or their allies in the main waterway, but some of them were already developing in the sheltered swamps which are a hatchery for certain kinds early in the year. Every week now will bring a noticeable change of scene here and it will become difficult to keep track of all that is happening, but today it was just possible to glimpse the subtleness of spring's first assault on winter's fortress.

Suffolk Coast

Surlingham, April 1st, 1951

We visited a lonely spot on the Suffolk coast today, tramping first along the beach below cliffs that had been newly scoured by storms so that their lamination of clay and completely bedded sand, and the chocolate-coloured band of iron-bound soil underlying the bracken roots exposed at their top, looked almost artificially neat, like a geographer's model.

Presently we reached a point where the cliffs came to an end and Covehithe Broad lay just behind a slight ridge of shingle over which the sea had been sweeping recently. We had noticed quantities of cuttle-bones washed up to the foot of the cliffs, and now a very curious unusual vista lay before us; hundreds of ivory white cuttle-bones shone like great water lily petals where they had floated into the reed beds on the broad after being swept over the dividing beach on a big tide. Were the process of erosion along that part of the coast to be reversed, how puzzling the presence of all these cuttle-fish would be to some future geologist studying the reedy peats of the broad.

Returning by way of the cliff top, we saw many gorse bushes which had been so regularly nibbled by rabbits that they had assumed a compact form of growth. Some resembled turfy ant hills while others looked like green sand castles, stalagmites, ruined churches and pre-historic monuments. Some of these grotesque mounds had a single prickly wand protruding from them. Some of the gorse had been burnt and the scorched ground was now covered with a crimson carpet of almost microscopically small plants of sheep's sorrel.

A Tiny Stream

Surlingham, April 2nd, 1951

Islands and isolated patches of water have an equal fascination for the naturalist in that inhabitants of each must be accounted adventurers. Coconuts drift to coral atolls far out in the Pacific and become palms; the reed-mace fluffs its featherweight seeds into the air and colonises pools in every quarter of the globe. A new concrete pond in a garden is quickly peopled by water boatmen, water beetles and water weeds of various kinds without human assistance, just as a new volcanic peak thrusting its way out of the ocean depths becomes verdant with trees, ferns and mosses and alive with birds and insects in the course of a few years.

The other day I came upon a tiny stream which emerged from a spring in a Suffolk cliff and soaked away in the sand of the beach just below. Despite the extreme brevity of its course, this waterway was inhabited by a rich variety of plants and animals characteristic of streams in general. It had one peculiar feature: all its thousands of little water snails were of a special dwarf variety of a single species, known as Jenkins' spire-snail. This is the only British mollusc in which every individual is able to reproduce its kind parthenogenetically, and it appears almost certain that all the snails in the stream originated from a single dwarf ancestor which found its way there by accident some years ago.

As Beauty Unfolds

Philosophy, like St. Elmo's Fire,
　　Flickers in darksome places,
Tempting poor artists to a mire,
　　Shaming their frantic faces.
Have none of it, but, fancy free,
　　Be bold to face the wonder
Of a lone spirit, just to see
　　If Fate or you will blunder.
Art is a toss and tumble game,
　　Yet sweet and grave employment,
Vari-interpreting the same
　　To multiply enjoyment.
Did ever artist shed a tear
　　Upon a secret painting?
I doubt he ever felt a fear
　　But of his brush a-feinting!
When sunbeams dance upon a nose
　　And eyes just fail to focus,
Objective thoughts refuse to pose;
　　But is this hocus-pocus?
When crystal eye meets crystal eye
　　All being is all seeing
(And then to daub's to slowly die
　　And scribe a graph in fleeing).
Tradition is a witch-priest's child,
　　Bridesmaid to Truth and Vision;
With star-dust she may both beguile
　　And bring about collision.
But, Critic! Beauty's more than Truth:
　　'Tis Truth with understanding
(Though haloes ring the quite uncouth
　　While Truth demands unhanding).
Let artists all with passion strive
　　To sublimate a meaning
And with their darling tools contrive
　　The Spirit's perfect weaning.

At Sundown

Surlingham, April 13th, 1951

After a day of gusts and showers peace fell upon us at sundown and as a last bright ribbon of fire along the western rim of the fields gave way to greyness beneath the evening star, I listened to birds trilling from the leafless tres, toads croaking from the dykes, snipe drumming invisibly from the air above and tawny owls making strange music from mysterious places far and near.

Standing by a fallen birch log which had become richly caparisoned with frills of bracket-fungi through long sojourning in grass and heather, I noticed the silver beading of every green blade and the soft sheen of smoothly washed earth in little islands where the rain had subdued a hundred mole hillocks.

Presently a white owl came from the east and hung in the air for a moment facing me as it turned in flight and we looked at one another in what I felt to be a slight embarrassment. Then the owl passed swiftly on noiseless wings into the woods, following a bracken-filled glade in line with a hollow tree, to which I suspect he repaired without delay to meditate upon his strange encounter.

An Insect Disaster

Eccles, September 2nd, 1951

I don't know how much, if any, of the parish of Eccles remains unengulfed by the sea. My one-inch Ordnance map omits its very name; but the beach at any rate must belong, for under it lies the last of Eccles Church. Happily erosion has abated along this part of the coast for the time being, though the cliffs just northward are still receding fast. Here the groynes have helped to build up the beach, and a sea wall constructed only a few years ago is already almost hidden by blown sand capped by a flourishing growth of marram and other sand-binding grasses. Most of the bungalows which could be seen easily from the shore are now hidden from view by the new dunes, and the winter tide-mark shows as a line of prickly saltwort, sea rocket and other maritime plants growing well to seaward of the protective bank.

Early this morning I watched swallows and sand martins coasting northward here, while small groups of common terns did likewise over the sea. As the sun's warmth increased millions of common ladybirds climbed the marram grass and took wing, together with other small insects, while various kinds of

wandering butterflies, including large and small Whites, Brimstones, Peacocks, Small Tortoiseshells and Wall Browns, appeared. Many of these insects flew out to sea during the morning helped by the offshore breeze. Then the wind changed and the evening tide brought in masses of them drowned and half-drowned in a long black line frothy with foam. There were vast numbers of weevils, black flies and hover flies, many devil's coach-horse beetles, green tortoise beetles, ladybirds and daddy-longlegs, several common pond-skaters, shield bugs and water-boatmen, silver-Y moths, a peacock butterfly, grasshoppers, wasps, bees, caddis flies, winged ants and sawflies, in all amounting to more than a hundred species.

A Frayel of Woad

Surlingham, December 6th, 1951

In East Anglia we call a basket made of bulrushes a 'frail.' Being curious about the origin of this name some time ago, I found that it was derived from an old French word 'frayel' for the same thing; but more recently I came upon some very early instances of its use in this part of the country in connection with the ancient woad industry which was of considerable importance in Eastern England from the 13th century until the end of the 18th century, when the importation of indigo brought about its decline.

It appears that French merchants were instrumental in introducing the cultivation of woad, which largely supplanted madder as a dye soon afterwards. It is recorded that woad was sold by the 'frayel' at Lynn in 1243 and at Norwich a few years later. It was sold by other weights and measures also and, indeed, there were local disputes concerning this until it was agreed before the 'King's Intinerant Justices' in 1286, that the merchants should be allowed to sell their woad by the coomb and bushel in Norwich, as well as to bring it into the city in 'frailles.'

The frail basket in those days must have been fairly capacious for the tax on the woad contained in it was the same as that of a full cask. It is interesting to recall that in Norfolk we stuck to the ancient pronunciation of 'wad' until quite recently and country wives only a generation ago were often heard to say badly washed and over-'blued' linen hung out by neighbours that it was as blue as wad.

In a Churchyard

Surlingham, April 9th, 1952

Country churchyards seem to be most beautiful when grass, daisies, wild daffodils and wandering ivy have healed their earthen scars and brought life and fragrance to the green acres set aside for meditation and remembrance. There one may marvel at the ant's labours and glimpse the quick-eyed lizard basking in the sun, while a wren pecks diligently at moss and lichens softly banked upon a time-worn slab of stone. The slow-worm there finds happiness in an oasis bounded safely from the dangerous road and the jolly toad seeks luxury there through the summer days.

Round about churchyards often enough tall elms provide accommodation for a rookery, while jackdaws people the church tower and hollow trees close by. One could write a natural history of churchyards, for they offer little opportunities to many plants and creatures, which mean peril of extermination outside their confines.

The sexton of a church not far from Norwich has just passed on a record of the special churchyard behaviour of a pair of turtle doves last spring. The birds built their nest entirely of wire from old wreaths which had been put aside in a corner, and the young were reared successfully on this uncomfortable platform.

On Hickling Broad

Surlingham, April 22nd, 1952

This afternoon I watched the play of muted sunlight and felt the breeze and splashing of chill rainstorms on Hickling, wildest of the Broads. A pale grey Montagu's Harrier cock battled with the wind and gained an erratic mastery as it flapped and sailed like a gull, and the next moment sheered away and hurtled neath the dark clouds like a piece of paper caught by a jolly roger.

Pied shoveller and sheldrake glittered in a perfect setting of silver light and gloom, and little garganey teal skimmed the reedy wastes with the smart, swift, curving wing stroke of lively waders. Redshanks piped in company with crying peewits, and on the rushy grazing levels later we found their spotted eggs in scoops close together.

Ringed plover whistled on a mud-patch and a small flock of dunlin sped across the water, flashing white as they turned. Bitterns boomed intermittently and sedge warblers churred restlessly in the reed and sedge which chafed with brittle sound themselves as the wind smote them in invisible waves of strength. Swallows darted in and out of a boat-shed over a dyke as a solitary cuckoo called in the distance. A barn owl flapped across the marsh in broad daylight; black-headed gulls screamed on high. Hickling, for all its tempest, was in a mood of high spring ecstasy and, as ever, an avian paradise.

Dance of the Gnats

Surlingham, May 17th, 1952

This evening towards sunset we took a boat down the Fen Channel and Rockland Fleet Dyke to the River Yare. After a day of blazing sunshine and sallow bushes were white with a silken burden of seeding catkins, from which the fluff was scudding continually. At a distance many of the bushes appeared as snowy as burgeoning thorns, and later, as dusk fell, drifting lines of fluff upon the waters, thick and luminous, with shoreward depths of darkness behind them, glistened like the forms of silvery boats that drift silently under the stars.

Before night came on we witnessed the aerial dance of gnats above the willow trees and sallow bushes along the Fleet. The insects were present in millions and swirled like clouds of black smoke against the blushing sky. Their performance much resembled that of great starling flocks wheeling over a reed roost. A column would shoot upwards, then swing out to form a tenuous spiral, packing again almost at once into a thick cloud and spinning to earth. From a little distance the effect was often much like that of the swiftly pulsating and shimmering lights of the aurora, and all the time the air was filled with the ecstatic music of a myriad small, screaming wings.

Natterjacks

Surlingham, June 6th, 1952

Last night we made an expedition to Reedham in the hope that we might see something of the natterjacks for which that riverside spot is famous. For as long as anyone can remember, the little emerald-eyed, yellow-striped running toads have had their burrows in the cliff-like sandy terrace ground close to the banks of the Yare, where local gardeners cherish them, as well they may, for their persistent slug-catching and destruction of many insect pests.

Unfortunately, with modern developments along the water front and the increase of traffic and human activity generally, the natterjack colony has become depleted of late, but these very attractive little amphibians are still fairly numerous and well known in the village.

We arrived in mid-evening and were told to wait until dusk for the tuning-up of natterjack voices along the edge of the river where spawning was in progress amongst reeds in shallow, muddy tide pools. Just before ten o'clock we heard the ventriloquial rattling voices, at first mingled with the songs of lark and reed warblers; then, in a strange pulsating chorus, interrupted only by the tremulous music of a wood owl far away. The joyful toads had found a breeding ground to their liking on the wild uncivilised side of the river and must have crossed its salty waters to get there.

Coypus   1953 ?

Otters affecting fledglings
1998

Hickling Broad   T. Ellis.   (1952)
Bitterns   Surlingham April 22   Pg 39
+ many species ecstatic.

Reindeer Moon

The moss is silvered in the glade
   This gentle night
And ferns like phantom wreaths are laid
   In secret light.
A reindeer moon rides in the sky
   And crystal frost
Crisps leaves to tinsel as they lie
   On paths embossed
With patterns of a travelled way.
   Aside, I see
Pricked out with stars unknown to day,
   A holly tree:
Its berries mutely flushed with peace.
   An ivy cloak
Steals radiance of a golden fleece
   From gilded oak
And from its folds a weird flute
   Wavers away —
A brown owl's tremulous salute
   And solemn say.
Great trees tonight a cloister make
   And standing here
Beneath the reindeer moon, I take
   Thought of the year

(1953)

Beside the Sea

Surlingham, June 29th, 1952

Today we spent a few hours at the seaside just north of Lowestoft, bathing in a calm blue sea and lazing afterwards on a burning beach. All the time larks soared and sang high above the cliffs and even out over the sea, lost to sight in the dazzling radiance of a summer sky. Well out from the shore, little terns kept flashing southwards on fast beating wings, out-stripping the gulls which journeyed the same way.

We kept watch for a possible immigration of white butterflies, but saw none of these adventurers flutter over the water. Once in a while we spotted a brown-looking butterfly approaching the shore at great speed, but the only arrival identified with certainty was a small tortoiseshell, which darted and planed close to the hot sand, revealing its bright wing pattern for a moment before it shot upwards over the cliff.

The strong southward flow of the tidal current was revealed by a drifting object off shore; it looked like a monster porcupine, but we decided that it was a much travelled 'hover' of reeds and a jagged limb of a tree which must have been carried out to sea from a Broadland river.

As the tide rose over the sloping beach the gently lapping waves brought in thousands of sea-gooseberries—small gooseberry-shaped jellyfish which as they swam displayed irridescent lines of colour and trailed long pale tentacles. Presently they lay stranded, like so many crystal pebbles, and at the turn of the tide we knew that the heat of the sun would wither their beauty to vanishing point, leaving scarcely a raindrop impression upon the sand.

The Morris Dancers

Oxford, July 22nd, 1952

Yesterday I journeyed through the sunlit countryside to this city of matured beauty, and after speeding past bright cornfields of white and gold at the threshold of harvest, parched meadows, heat-weary towns and a million scattered trees yet gracing the winding highways of England, came at last to the peace that dwelt eternally within a college garden.

Here, in the quiet of evening, I squatted on a vast ancient lawn to watch a performance of Morris dancing while ring-doves soared and swifts sped through the summer air above and gargoyles in strange array looked down from the castellated and creepered facade of a neighbouring college hall. Presently the Morris men walked on rather like a team of cricketers. They wore dark blue jockey caps, white shirts cross ribboned red and blue, and fawn trousers with red and blue leg pads on which were stitched rows of little brass bells. For some of their dances they carried short wooden staves. Accompanying them was a kind of clown or jester very differently arrayed. He wore a foolish hat of soft brown felt, plumed and beribboned red and blue from which an untidy fore-lock protruded with great effect; a yellow neckerchief smock, buff knickerbockers, one stocking red and the other blue, and a pig bladder tied to a stick completed his equipment. Music from a concertina was provided by an ancient Morris man who sat in a chair, a serene and twinkling master of ceremony.

To jigging, skirling tunes the dancers stepped out and in, weaving lively patterns and making dumb show. They made a mockery of sowing beans and swaggering, and all the time the lilt of English music and I think older music from far off hills in wildest Europe enlivened their frolics while the jester made capers and used his wacking bauble to distract the dancers and keep the audience in merry mood.

Whooper Swans

Surlingham, December 2nd, 1952

One morning during the past week we were awakened soon after five o'clock by the trumpet notes of whooper swans as the great birds flew just above our house in brilliant moonlight.

There is magic in the wild night music of pipers on the mud-flats, peewits skirling on stony fields, curlews travelling high above the silver river, and grey geese loudly gossiping and squabbling on their journeys to and from the coast. There is mystery in many a strange cry, squeak or whistle heard in the fog of an autumn night when migrant birds are on the move in their thousands. There is pure glory in the whispering, trilling, fluting chorus that welcomes the day's awakening in spring. There is poignancy in the strange utterances of

all fowls of the air at times when they are rejoicing in domestic bliss and coquetry. A signal of ancestral fear is aroused by the screeching and wailing of owls when night clouds ink the skies and the pollard oak assumes distorted human shapes. But in all my experience of bird music, never have I heard anything so deeply stirring as the bold and measured trumpet blasts of those moon-silvered swans when they swept so close to us as to disturb our slumbers all unwittingly the other morning.

Burgh Castle Find

Surlingham, April 5th, 1953

Towards the close of this chill and windy Easter Day we enjoyed a brief adventure at Burgh Castle, in sunshine which of a sudden swept the vast arena of the marshlands about Breydon and created a great unexpected glory after grey North Sea clouds had frowned upon the hopes of spring too long. As we strolled down the narrow hill from the church a vista of sparkling water, golden reed beds, red sails in the sunset and innumerable birds with flashing wings lay before us, while away towards Yarmouth stretched the once green grazing marshes, now curiously brown after their recent drowning in sea water.

Presently, to the tune of redshank pipers, we turned along the marsh path below a hanging cliff, intending to reach the Roman fortress quickly and to see its flint and brickwork beautified by the dipping sun. But haste was out of the question, for it soon became apparent that at the foot of the cliff beneath blossoming cherry-plums and budding thorn-trees something interesting had occurred as a result of the sea's February inburst. A tide line of reedy rubbish and a narrow sandy beach showed where the waves had licked the base of this inland cliff, washing out not only the natural boulder clay, gravel and sand, but also the brown earth with whatever human spoil it might contain.

So we found ourselves launched on a treasure hunt along the little beach half hidden and until now untrampled beneath the bushes. We were rewarded by finding an assortment of roman potsherds scattered along the whole length, together with the shells of oysters and whelks, and bones of domestic animals cast away by inhabitants of the ancient camp near by.

Beauty by a Beck

Surlingham, May 20th, 1953

This evening I paused for a few minutes along the Norwich-Loddon turnpike at Framingham to enjoy a glimpse of the favourite beck which trickles over its bed of pebbles between deep and steep banks clothed with a most glorious assemblage of wild flowers in spring.

There I looked down on lily-white umbel-heads of ramsons, the broad-leaved garlic of moist, shady places, and viewed tier upon tier of the pale gold, hooded blossoms of arch-angel peeping between nettle-like leaves of rich and shining salad green. The foliage of familiar wayside plants such as hogweed, stinging nettles, dock and nipplewort, with lush tufts of grasses, formed a mosaic pattern of great beauty, in a dappling of sunshine and darkest shade.

A white lacing of hedge parsley in flower beside the road was matched in delicacy by galaxies of white stitch-wort flowers upon the farther bank and huge white dead-nettles mass-ed beneath. Here and there the strange dank spathe of a wild arum lurked in the shadows with sprawling fern-like leaves and magenta flowers of herb robert for company.

The jaundice-flower of the gypsies, the great celandine of opiate affinity with the poppies, had found a luxurious footing in the depths. I could have lingered much longer in this place of botanical delights and as I travelled on, temptation came again and again to stop by some ivied brick culvert or one of the many beautiful groups of trees along the course of the beck, that I might sample the riches of another vista and share a little longer the joy of all the singing birds along that way.

Noises in Moonlight

Surlingham, June 20th, 1953

Tonight I went on the water by moonlight, savouring all the delicious scents of the fen flowers and grasses born of the day's warmth and the distilling of dew. There was even a pleasant, almost seashore, tang in the smell of mud and waterweeds stirred by my punt paddle as I touched the shallows. Yellow irises flanked the dykes like pale torches held aloft by unseen hands. Glowworms twirled greenish lights in the grasses.

Coypus sat on shore eyeing me quietly within an oar's length when I slipped by silently on the ebb tide; but when I splashed the water they plunged and swam in a zig-zag course ahead of the punt until overtaken, then made upstream and landed where they belonged.

Here and there I startled a heron and he startled me with hoarse and almost gutteral swearing, Flapper ducklings scurried ahead, leaving an agitated wake in the Fen Channel; then, warned by an anxious parent, they used their wings as best they could and crashed through a reed bed to get out of the way.

Bats dipped low to snatch mosquitoes which followed the boat in a moving column above my head. Redshanks piped musically on the marshes and along the muddy shores. I found Rockland Broad peaceful with moonbeams flashing on the gently rippled waters. A brief murmur of conversation in the distance betokened the presence of eel-babbers whiling away the hours of mystery.

Into the Wash

King's Lynn, July 13th, 1953

Today I voyaged from Lynn across the Wash to the neighbourhood of the Sunk Buoy while the vast bay was all a lively, wind-whipped sea and rain smote our ship in dark squalls, hiding even the bold features of Snettisham's Ken Hill and the chocolate-and-cream sandwich cliffs of Hunstanton from view much of the time.

At intervals during the morning small migratory parties of swifts battled their way south-westwards through the rain, keeping close to the surface of the water and once in a while we glimpsed the bewhiskered face of a seal as it surfaced.

We trawled on a sandy shelf of the sea bed known as the Common and our sample haul contained thornback rays, young skate, soles, gobies, pogges, a little squid, sea-gooseberry jellyfish, shore crabs, swimming crabs known as 'fliers' and various kinds of starfish.

In the afternoon we made our way up the new main channel and saw the tide fall away from the great banks and flats of sand and mud. Landing on the Pandora Sand, we walked a vast distance to examine the mussel-scaups. It is estimated that there are 9000 tons of mussels in the Wash, where they grow to plumpness quickly.

We found small acorn barnacles coating their shells in millions and at low levels, starfish were hunched up on some of them, sucking the entire shellfish out by force. We saw drifts of bleached cockle shells and huge clams and vast numbers of lug-worm casts, little shell-grit-fingered tubes of Terebella worms and wet holes made by clams.

The weather improved as we journeyed upstream to Lynn and towards the west we looked across a sweep of sand which shone like hammered silver beyond the black-stepped scoured shore of the channel. Willows and poplars on the far-off tree line were silhouetted like a mirage in the desert. Eastward, a new grassy sea wall was illuminated by a sweep of sunlight so that it appeared like a turquoise line against the darkness of the wooded hills beyond.

September's Night

Surlingham, September 7th, 1953

At the close of this summery September day, the orange glow of sunset faded but slowly in a clear sky. The earth gave up its warmth to the upper air and long before the light had died a chill mist began to brood over the meadows. It came first as an almost imaginary gossamer to be traced now here, now there, as an unsubstantial mirage or the shifting curtain of pale aurora light; then as a thickening fleece of fairy snow through which could be seen the softened contours of mole-hills and out of which peeped the tips of rushes darkling and separate.

The air, to all feeling, was perfectly inert and no single leaf trembled upon a tree, yet the mist played strange tricks before my eyes. It advanced and receded, thickened and shrank, hovered in detached lens-shaped strata and, in fact, played will o' the wisp almost magically in the changing light.

Presently, four peewits appeared on the scene. They swooped skirling as they skimmed the surface of the mist and for a few minutes enacted a wild play before me. Then they alighted on the meadow and were at once silent and still beneath their white covering.

Small bats fluttered round but kept well out of the mist. I heard the deep droning of more than one black dor-beetle abroad over the meadow, but otherwise the field of the cloth of silver was as serene as the face of a winter's moon when I left it in the dusk.

Autumn's Mirror

Surlingham, September 24th, 1953

The red, the purple and the gold of autumn's leafy splendour are mirrored already in the waters of the Fen. The slender reed mace of the swamp is yellow as wheat amongst the green pennants and silvering plumes of reed.

Tints of rose, magenta and wine, of scarlet, bronze, orange and saffron streak and fleck the feathery fronds of waterside umbellifers. Spent meadowsweep, gypsywort, wild black currant and many a small marsh herb. Here and there a guelder rose bush stands like a beacon of crimsoned fire with every leaf aglow and every branch heavy with ruby-bright berries.

The sallows have not begun to lose their leaves, but some are black with sooty moulds, some prematurely yellowed by rust fungi and yet others becoming flecked with brown and gold through simple weariness of their sap.

Spear leaves of iris are ragged and streaked with black. The nut-brown seed-heads of milk parsley stand on high above the green and graceful sedge tussocks. As the alder leaves drop from branch after branch it is possible to see more of the silver filigree of lichen on forked twigs in between.

With the rising of every morning mist now, some new loveliness appears in the transformation scene about this watery stage, where the Harlequin and Columbine are the mallard and his mate.

Gipsy

Gipsy dressed in yallery gold,
　　Parchment-faced and jaundiced, old,
Like an oriole you flash,
　　With amber beads and silken sash
And sunbeams sparkling on your rings
　　As on daffodils of a thousand springs.
Deep in your heart a fire glows,
　　Warming a way through winters' snows.
Sunflower of burning noon,
　　Luminous as a Harvest Moon:
Dignity of ancient race
　　Lightens your step, shines in your face.
You are a queen in a captive land
　　Where everything but freedom's planned.
Envy would steal the last green stance
　　Where a gipsy child might hope to dance;
But when the World is jaundiced, old,
　　May you reign here still, in yallery gold.

(1953)

A Smoke of Starlings

Surlingham, September 25th, 1953

Looking eastward a little before sunset this evening, we perceived a smoke of starlings in the sky above Rockland Broad. It was a smoke which rose in thin black columns, swirled, shuddered, dissolved, formed itself into flying saucer shapes, descended like rain, became a series of smudges, scudding in circles and rose again in curtains, spirals and dark jets like weird waterspouts.

From afar we could hear the swishing of twenty thousand wings and the shrill gossip and whistling of ten thousand throats. But this was not enough—we slipped down the Fen Channel fast on the falling tide, to be in time to see the starling express come in.

As we reached the Broad, a sound exactly like the hissing of a mighty engine rose from the reed beds about us. As flock after flock packed itself into the overburdened reeds and roared into the air in panic, it is no exaggeration to say that the impact of wings upon the reeds produced momentary thunder-claps.

Every whirling flock was mirrored in the water, for the surface of the Broad was smooth as glass and even the mist rising about the willows was reflected as a breath of beauty. We saw half a dozen crested grebes floating, perfectly still, with white necks erect seemingly awed and curious at the enactment of such strange rites.

Swallows twittered above us until after sundown. The starlings settled at last and bats came forth over the water as the moonbeams filtered through the greying sky.

The Gale in the Fen

Surlingham, January 3rd, 1954

We were awakened in the early hours of this morning by a sudden roaring onrush of wind which smote the woods and passed on like an express train into the distance. This was the herald blast which ushered in a day of chill unease.

Daybreak revealed a wintry sky and thereafter the north wind lashed the countryside with squalls of hail and sleet. One could see dark cascades falling from the cloud mountains and from time to time a play of rainbows added majesty to the scene. Many birds, unprepared for such a sudden change of fortune, took to skulking and sheltering in bushes and reed-beds. None flew farther than was absolutely necessary, and flocks of starlings and fieldfares broke up into small companies, obviously harassed by their buffeting.

Water birds sought the more secluded pools and sheltered bays and even the swans gathered in a close pack on a small sheet of water in the lee of a carr.

This afternoon I toured the marsh country of the Lower Yare and Waveney, sharing a watch on the swollen tide as it tested the flood banks. I disturbed peewits in the green pastures behind river walls; even these birds of exposed moorland were shrinking from the gale. The one blithe spirit met with on my travels was a pied wagtail. He took a cold bath then spread his tail and wings to dry in the all but freezing wind, twittering happily all the time.

The Wind's Orchestra

Surlingham, January 19th, 1954

Tonight we followed the advice tendered in the old adage: 'After supper walk a mile.' Rubber-booted, we set out across a squelching fen beloved of glow-worms in summer. After brushing through a stiff, brittle growth of meadowsweet and rushes, we breasted our way through wind-swept seas of reed and reed-grass, fitfully pale and dark as the clouds racing overhead thinned and thickened their veil shrouding the moonlight

From time to time we stepped into black-mires and softly gleaming pools beneath the fen alders. The rounded humps of sallow bushes with their fine twigs bristling looked rather like giant hedgehogs. A mild but boisterous breeze bent everything before it and the hissing grating of dry stalks and crisp crackling leaves and the gusty soughing and whispering of trees and bushes combined to produce a sound like that of storm surf breaking on a lonely shore.

In contrast to a stilly night, when birds and nocturnal mammals break the silence and the spell with nervous outcries again and again, all creatures are hushed when the wind rouses its rattle-bone orchestra in the wilds of Broadland.

Calm at Evening

Surlingham, May 26th, 1954

This evening we spent an hour idling on quiet waterways with the fragrance of the sun-warmed fen about us. The first yellow iris gleamed among the green spear leaves and the first creamy outer blossoms of the guelder-rose showed as pale circles, rather like suspended haloes in the shadow-land of bushes overhanging the water.

The cuckoo called, the turtle dove crooned in the thickets and a bittern uttered its deep booming notes far away in the reeds towards the river.

Thousands of water-flies were performing their ritual dances, shuttling back and forth in rhythmic races. We found the sallow bushes bright with cotton-tail catkins, prinked out with glistening fluff. Some of the fluff was festooned in spiders' webs between the branches; much more was drifting like snow blossoms of fairyland upon the waters.

We slipped by the great tussock sedges, now magnificent with drooping flower heads of brown and gold. There were other sedges some with buff plumes like cockades; others with green and black zebra patterns on their fruiting spikes.

We bruised sweet-scented flags in the narrows and peered at the delicate fronds of marsh ferns uncurling in dark places. We saw the white cuckoo flower of the swamps and the yellow rocket topping some of the green floating islands. As mallard rose from the swamps, they left some of their small pencilled feathers behind on the water, showing that their summer moult had begun.

Coming home by the main dyke at sundown, we found large pearls of dew tipping the grass blades; the buttercup flowers were closed in sleep and the first breath of night mist was curling like smoke from the water.

June Magic

Surlingham, June 16th, 1954

Many people like myself must have enjoyed resting under a greenwood tree in the heat of this glorious June day. With my head pillowed on bracken, I gazed into the gold and green and silver traceries of the treetops, sparkling and translucent against the blue of the sky.

I realised that many years had passed since I had looked at trees topsy-turvy. The sky became a mirror, a still unfathomable pool reflecting the snow-bright wands of silver birches, meandering boughs of hornbeam and oak, great sprays of leaves flung into the heavens like the airy spume of fountains and little crests of leaves, dazzling as silvered peaks of mountains far off.

The sun was away at an angle burning bold shadows across the glades and filling the tree-top world with splendour. Little golden hover flies were suspended in space, as in a dream of fairies, darting and floating playfully in the twinkling realm of leaves and sunbeams. The incense of bracken and pine needles was warm about me, but no fragrance descended from the high-perched clusters of honeysuckle—this would come down with the dew at the day's end.

Birds were silent and still; the peace of a steaming jungle seemed to have fallen upon this corner of an English wood suddenly bewitched.

Act of Adoration

Surlingham, July 6th, 1954

This is the month of honeysuckle, and as the moon waxes there will be the year's one marvellous chance for observing the adoration of giant hawk moths where the pale sweet blossoms hang upon the trees.

Already the night air is heavy with their spicy fragrance. They are suspended like wreaths of waxen satin-bright orchids in the depth of a tropical rain forest. The flowers point in all directions, forming rings of friendly inviting faces. The night air may grow chill and the dew all but freeze in the stilly hour before dawn, but the sweetness of woodbine, like the distillation of sweet briar, becomes the keener for its purifying.

The great moths swoop out of the shadows like creatures from another world. Their haste, their silence, the delicacy of their brief act of worship before each flower face—all seem quite magical to the beholder under the moon.

This is a good season for hawk moths, and in all seriousness I would like to suggest that, as a change from going out to listen to the dawn chorus or to hear the nightingale's nocturne or to look at the glow-worms twirling their little lanterns in the grass, those in search of a gentle adventure go seek the honeysuckle presently and wait for the ghostly moths.

Awake in Dreamland

Surlingham, October 13th, 1954

It may be scientifically possible to attain silence; but in nature, even in the quietude of night, one can at least hear the music of the spheres in whispers as a faint song of the sea within a shell.

Here, in what may be described truly as a lonely place in the backwoods, I am aware of the hush which has fallen since the rest of the family has retired to sleep; but now the weary bluebottle behind a curtain makes a little flurry of a buzz and I find myself listening to the whining of mosquitoes on their exploratory travels.

The ticking clock presides over this peace within and I have only to listen outwards, so to speak, to realise that the wind is bearing steadily upon the woods tonight and creating the same noble sound as water pouring over a weir.

The fire pops. I rustle and creak a little myself. I step outside for a moment. Owls are not in festive mood tonight and there are no wild alarums from flesh or fowl, in all the world of clouded moonlight. but earthworms are scratching and snapping beneath the dewy grass, tempted forth by the mildness of the air, and field voles are munching verdure.

It may be that there is some gentle music out of my reach in the beatings of moths' wings and the sailing of dry autumn leaves towards their mossy resting places. So I find my imaginings and the gentle realities combine most pleasantly and I am awake in that dreamland wherein elves and fairies come to life, to make merry.

The Rainbow's End

Surlingham, November 15th, 1954

I spent a short time today in the bleak, flat marsh country that lies northward of the river beyond King's Lynn. The sun had but newly dispersed the chill vapours of night and the turf was still frozen in the hollows of marshland pastures.

I saw the vast moving cloudscape to perfection across the open land, and realised that in the changing beauty of the heavens those that dwelt in the comparative desolation of reclaimed fen and mudflat found recompense for their isolation.

How warm a thing was a homestead there, touched by the autumn sunlight as by a torch, against the grey sweep of a hailstorm cloud. On a day such as this the full brave span of a rainbow was indeed a Sign in the darkling sky.

The people of Terrington, Tilney and Clenchwarton might not be stirred to look for a pot of gold at the rainbow's end; but one felt that they or their like must have been moved long ago to suggest the existence of such treasure.

The land is not altogether without the intricate charm of trees; it has its willows by water here and there and I saw some glorious hawthorns spaced out along some of the roads. These thorns, grown as trees, were crowned with a wealth of crimson berries, and today vast flocks of fieldfares were plundering them with riotous enjoyment.

A Winter's Curse

Surlingham, December 8th, 1954

As I came home tonight, funereal clouds were banked across the moon: not brooding clouds, but monsters, humping their way in sullen procession like whales pursuing Jonah. Towards the south, a pale defiant light swept through the heavens, where moonbeams struggled in far outposts of their realm and touched the storm with beauty. And soon a rage of wind crashed on the trees. Thunder and lightning broke into violent symphony; a winter's curse fell on a cowering land and beat it dead with hail.

Out of the wood a witch's stewpot bird, a crow tumbled in fear and croaked thrice, like a raven. Leaves beat upon my window—last leaves wrenched like the crow from their branch hold in a crazed wilderness. The great squall passed; the wind sighed like the sea and seahorse clouds rode on a star-pricked ocean sky. Far lightning winked at the moon as she sailed in a fret of spindrift. After five minutes, I looked again; the moon was all besieged and impotent; outriders of another storm smothered her face with cloaks of mourning. The music of the sky was overborne by furies and the rage of Thor returned.

Secret Paradise

Surlingham, April 17th, 1955

This afternoon we made our way through the green lanes of primrose country to the Bath Hills of Ditchingham, there to be bewitched by the gentle Waveney, the far-rimmed plain of Outney Common and the strange steep slopes of tree-clad inland cliffs.

We had the feeling that we had invaded a secret paradise, a lost valley, a rare new Norfolk, so lovely and so enfolding the life and sunlight within it that it seemed almost unreal.

A nightingale was out-singing the little summer warblers amongst the green buds of the hillside trees. Peacock butterflies were flopping upon open flowers and travelling with exploratory mien across the haunts of nettle and red campion.

We were specially delighted to see some of the rare plants of the hills still flourishing some century and a-half after they had been noticed by Daniel Stock, the Bungay botanist, and recorded by him in works on the British Flora. Thus the green, purple-tipped flowers of stinking hellebore were attracting honeybees everywhere amongst the trees and the papery spear leaves of gladdon the wild purple iris were even more abundant tufting the steep ground.

Meditations in a London Street on a Sunny September Day

All the centuries are here, and all the world:
   Gentleman in a flowered gown, from darkest Africa;
Petunias, trumpets of beauty from the Indian west
   Lodged in the dusty courts of Uxbridge;
And tropic splendour glowing where peppers, green and scarlet,
   Monstrous yams and aubergines, invite the curious eye.
A cosmos, too, in gay apparel: a blossoming of Art in human choice,
   Fluid and spangled as a stream.
A golden day renews a Golden Age.
   Swishing of locks, rustle of frocks;
A poetry of freedom wakes and breathes;
   Sunburst and shadow, a gliding pram;
The grace and courage of women;
   Youth and Age in harmony;
And pulsing over all
   The drums of destiny, half-silenced,
Like music from the stars.

I had been invited by the B.B.C. to take part in a Nationwide programme together with Malcolm Muggeridge and Cliff Richard. Arriving in London I had time on my hands and wandered into Uxbridge Road where a cosmopolitan scene inspired these thoughts.

The main carpet of undergrowth consisted of dog's mercury with lesser celandine, star-spangling the hem by the river. There, with the celandines, we saw the little birds'-eyes which had colonised much of the moist ground and which were mentioned as recent invaders by Miss Rider Haggard in her 'Countrywoman's Letter' last week; these were *Veronica filiformis*, native to the Middle East, and spreading rapidly in some parts of England.

Otters' Lairs

Surlingham, April 25th, 1955

We seldom see our restless, sportive otters, but that they are by no means scarce here is evident not only from the tracks they leave upon the snow in winter, but also from the fact that they leave many a trace of their fish suppers on the banks of our waterways.

Once in a while we hear an otter's remarkable whistle or catch a glimpse of a silver coated, seal-like creature frolicking and curvetting in the water by moonlight as we sit babbing for eels in the Fen Channel. There is a certain well-worn track in the marshes here said to have been used by otters for as long as anyone can remember. Coypus are using it today, but I saw it myself long before there were any coypus inhabiting the Yare Valley.

Yesterday some friends exploring our back-waters came upon two otters nests or 'holts' made of grasses and sedges amongst the roots of old alder trees. These contained fish scales suggesting that the creatures were in the habit of taking at least some of their food home to be consumed in comfort. These well-made nests are couches occupied by otters by day and not necessarily every day, for the beasts are said to have several alternative lairs which may be situated some miles apart.

Evening Clouds

Surlingham, August 8th, 1955

When the sky is a hazy blue on long summer days, we are little apt to explore its dazzling heights or, indeed, think very much about it. Nor does the light of a day-dreaming sky reveal the rich contrasting beauty of landscape, except in hill country, where shadows always play on a grand scale.

As I passed through the countryside between here and the coast this evening, dark piles of clouds hung in the amber heights, the arc of a rainbow spread its broad ribbon of delight before me, the corn fields were white unto harvest, the very hedge banks were crested with the flaxen-gold of dry, unkempt grasses, the trees were bold and dark and in the far smudged horizon I saw the threshold of Valhalla, the coast of Thule, the kirtle of the Universe.

The slowly moving storms were steeds for the heroic figures of mythology. The world below lay like a bright and fertile kingdom, cherished and blessed with all the yearning and achievement of man and nature consummated in its beauty.

We are happy in the sun but it takes the darkling imagery of evening clouds to awaken the immortal in us.

The Fenland Scene

Surlingham, December 4th, 1955

A few days ago, I drove through dismal fog from Norwich to Wisbech. On the last few miles of my journey the sky cleared and the Fenland scene was suddenly warmed to life. Canal-like channels intersecting the deeply-drained land mirrored the soft light of an autumn sky and reflected the flaming orange pennons of reeds here and there along their margins. Moorhens and dabchicks were crossing and recrossing these peaceful waterways at a number of points.

I saw rows of hawthorns bright with crimson berries, which had attracted a few wandering fieldfares and redwings. A magpie was preening his glossy breast on the crown of a golden weeping willow. A late yellow tansy flowered on a green verge. Tall umbels of wild parsnip stood on wayside banks, every detail of their form etched cleanly against the darkness of the fenland soil beyond them.

The rich black earth, overhung with lingering traces of mist, appeared blue-black from even a few yards away and quite blue in the distance, so that I came to realise for the first time how completely truthful Thomas Lound and other artists of the Fen Country had been in depicting their strangely blue misty landscapes, so different from familiar vistas of Broadland, the Breydon grazing levels or marshes of the North Norfolk coast.

Filby Broad

Surlingham, August 21st, 1956

A friend and I rowed on Filby Broad today and, after penetrating a slight barrier of reeds at the mouth of the Muckfleet, found our way to the small forgotten Broad of Burgh St. Margaret and its adjoining common. On the weedless waters of Filby we met with only two or three anglers settled in peaceful bays.

Great-crested grebes were much in evidence, some herring gulls were floating in the sunshine, and one of the common terns from the Broadland nesting colony in the neighbourhood was flying round and making an occasional dive for tiddlers.

Swallows skimmed low over the water, and occasionally settled in the reeds. It was noticeable that many of the bulrushes had turned yellow prematurely among their still green brethren. The sere specimens, when squeezed all the way up their stalks, were found to have little hard lumps in their pith formed by the parasitic fungus responsible for their dying back.

Along the shores of the Muckfleet we came upon several accumulations of freshwater mussel shells which had been dragged out by otters, one of which was swimming and diving near by. The dyke leading to Burgh Broad was lined with magnificent sedges, twig-topped with shining red-brown fruits. The bottom of the Broad seen through clear water looked like a rather weird submerged garden, with the spiky rosettes of water soldier visible at intervals like shadowy purple flowers.

Burgh Common was colourful with bog plants on its rough grazing, and along its sandy margin we saw the dwarf autumnal gorse in bloom, and noticed that its vicious prickles were curiously downy, unlike those of the ordinary gorse growing with it.

Sheer Ecstasy

Surlingham, September 22nd, 1956

This morning, after a night of thundery showers, the sun reigned over sparkling countryside, soon sweet with warm vapours from earth and leaves. Berries glowed on the hedgerows, purple knapweed attracted bees and butterflies, fat and gorgeous spiders sat in webs miraculously undamaged in the showery night.

I went up to the village and found a lively commotion going on in some high elms by the pond; starlings, glossy and iridescent in their new plumage, were hissing, whistling and cackling in ecstatic chorus. So might they have welcomed the true dawn of spring, or celebrated the end of a perfect summer's day in the reed-beds of Broadland.

The urgent gossip of a throng of starlings, halting and imperfect to a clownish degree, humbly trying but not triumphant, anarchic rather than regimented in its orchestration, is yet one of the sweetest expressions of happiness to be heard in all Nature.

Starlings chortle with the comfort of well-being as a child crows in the innocence of its earliest delights; they welcome the gift of a lovely morning with pure merriment, like a thousand untuneful errand boys, unabashed in the individuality of experimentation, riotously free of heart and prodigal with their poor talents.

Rare Dawn

Surlingham, January 17th, 1957

A rare winter's dawn transfigured the country-side this morning, a dawn with a rainbow misted against a sky of arctic blue and a zenith of snow clouds blushed with red corn gold.

The radiance of blue and gold found sympathy in all green things below. Never were England's fields a more dazzling green, and even the powdered tree trunks were pastelled in pale emerald. Road puddles flashed with the brilliance of kingfisher plumes and goldfish scales. Berries on the hedgerows glowed like rubies. Gulls soaring high were snow-white angel doves, emblems of purity bright against the indigo of the north.

On a height by Surlingham Church, I lifted small Susan to the top bar of a gate, that she might see with me the most beautiful valley in the world: a river dark beyond the scintillation of emerald turf, an enchanted forest with a white tower in its midst, a brown and crimson ribboning of hedgerows, a gateway to the sun.

It was then that a happy thought came to me. How splendid it would be if, all over the countryside, it were possible for us to mount the sentinel towers of our village churches at dawn and sunset for peaceful contemplation.

Waveney Valley

Surlingham, April 29th, 1957

Although an icy north-easter was blowing off the sea today, there was brilliant sunshine to engender warmth in sheltered places. We found such a haven in the Waveney Valley at Burgh Castle, where a wooded cliff of the old estuary kept most of the wind from a long strip of reedy rond and salt pools. Here was a vista of river walls white-capped and honey-scented, with flowers of scurvy-grass, of dazzling winter reeds and yellow-green pulks, of the silver blue sheet of Breydon Water with its curving banks and brown seaweed lines.

Butterflies were fluttering all about us; they were mostly green-veined whites looking for cresses, but there were also several large cabbage whites, peacocks and tattered small tortoiseshells. The pulks were dotted with tiny snails and full of wood-louse-like crustaceans (*Sphaeroma rugicauda*); mudflies were skimming the water without quite touching it and patches of dry, cracked mud were peopled by several kinds of glittering beetles and lively salt marsh bugs.

A yellow wagtail was busy snatching flies from the grass and the quarrel-some black-headed gulls were the only creatures to break the peace as they fought for something specially attractive in the way of food that was floating down the river. They were as noisy as a crowd of terns on Blakeney Point!

Moment of Magic

Surlingham, December 2nd, 1957

This morning's sun rose on a crystal world of frost, and as the day wore on its radiance dissolved the ice needles on lightsome boughs and repainted the world green except for the white shadows lingering behind bold hedges, woods, stacks and buildings.

The air remained very still most of the time, and one noticed only that it was cheerfully warm in the suntraps and bitterly cold in the shadows. During the morning, twigs and grass blades sweated and dripped, and by noon, steam could be seen rising here and there to contribute to the golden haze rimming the horizon.

While the sun was at its highest, I happened to look towards it across a square of fen which was bounded by woods on the south and west and in the midst of which stood a solitary pine tree. By shielding my eyes from the full glare, I was able to capture a moment of rare magic. A weirdly turbulent blue mist was swirling out of patches of meadowsweet near the pine tree and tent-like shadows cast by the boughs and brooms of pine needles showed in deep relief.

It was as though some witch, like a giant of the Brocken, stooped with her black cloak about her, tending a cauldron brew. This was not all the magic. Every plume of reed, every brown willow herb and spear of grass carried a glittering thread of gossamer which streamed out into the air twinkling like star-dust, flashing like sea-fire and occasionally waving in ripples like single strands of golden hair.

I saw no spider aeronauts, but winter gnats were jigging gently up and down in Tinker Bell dances, rising light as mist in the play of sunbeams.

Scolt Head Revisited

Surlingham, September 4th, 1958

Yesterday we crossed the rollicking green waters of Brancaster and tasted the salt spray many times before reaching Scolt Head Island. On the way we watched the graceful terns and listened to the musical piping of various wading birds; it was also amusing to see numerous bumble bees flying against the stiff sea breeze, keeping fairly close to the surface of the water as they went out to the beds of sea lavender on the tidal saltings.

Landing on the lateral ridge called Butcher's Beach, where the shingle is held fast by shrubby suaeda bushes and other tufting plants, we notice that the alien mud-binding rice-grass had produced a green jungle on much of the Cockle Bight since our last summer visit of a few years ago. Another plant which showed a marked increase was the entirely yellow-flowered variety of the sea aster which seems to be ousting the blue-rayed type on many stretches of salt marsh.

Rabbits have been almost exterminated on the island, with the result that there are now fewer 'scalt' patches on the dunes. Sand sedge and the finer grasses now grow tall and seed freely.

We picked up a dead cock redstart among the marrams– one of the many small migrants travelling westwards along this coast in the past few days. A chiffchaff crossed the water and skulked close to us as we were about to leave at the end of the afternoon.

We walked back over the sea lavender to Burnham Norton calling at a sandy point known as The Nod, to see if all was still well with Norfolk's only colony of the great sea rush. It came as a curious surprise when we found that the chestnut-brown flower-heads of the rush were all thickly covered with hairy-legged mining bees (*Dasypoda hirtipes*), a species which burrows in the sand of that part of the coast.

59

Night Comes to Town

Like cowelled monks
    Old gables hood the dusk.
Star windows wink
    And coral fires of lamps
Necklace the streets.
      Interstices
Of darkness curtain all
    And jungle shades bewitch
Familiar avenues to night.
     Day's dust is cooled
In dew distilled like spice,
    Wild in the nostril
And waking nerves
    To primal magic.
Now, cats are queens
    In No-Man's Land:
Come, let us make
    Carnival in painted halls,
Bugling and beating drums
    The night long,
Lest we may hear, too soon,
    The murmuring of stars.

Fantasies in Cloudland

Surlingham, September 30th, 1958

The whole sky was filled with wonders when I looked out just after sunset tonight. In the west, above the narrow band of sun fire dreamland cloud figures moved across the scene in turbulent procession.

It was like being in a vast aquarium and watching the approach of sharks and monsters through dimly-luminous waters; but in the nonsense of imagination, one saw shrimps, snakes and poodles drifting by inconsequentially, and dissolving into shapeless dusky vapours. There were curly 'dodman' clouds and the ragged 'water cart wheels', precursors of rain and for a time Neptune's hair streamed out in the current.

A blue zenith divided this realm of fantasies from another cloudland of a quite different mien in the east. There hung a mirage of gaunt highlands and lochs, with a far ridge of Alps, snow-capped and touched with faintest rose. Billows of lower clouds swirled by and descended like curling smoke as from the hills, completing the deception. A golden beech stood rustling at the bottom of the garden, and I grasped reality again when a duck darted out of the shadows, and when I stretched out a hand to touch white bellbine trumpets opening to the night. Two swallows raced southward in the darkness, and wild duck began to rise from the pools and make for the stubble lands. Presently the last dream of September faded and owls came out to quarrel under the moon.

Storm Mystery

Surlingham, June 30th, 1959

Nightfall came swiftly upon us at the close of this tropical day. The sky overhead, overcharged with the day's vapours, assumed a strange obscurity and away from the zenith it was tinged with the jaundice of ill-promise.

Then soft grey clouds, ragged heralds of storm, came whirling out of the west and straying this way and that, now hesitant, now agitated by demon winds. We saw black fingers, black crooked crosses, pale snakes like veins in black marble, blue peaks like mountains of lead.

The scene changed every minute with all the swift curtain shifting one associates more commonly with the aurora borealis and there were moments when the orange fire of distant lightning flared into the clouds and the similarity became closer still. As we waited to see whether the storm would break or perhaps send down the inky finger of a waterspout, there came a rushing wind followed by a tropical calm.

For us the omens seemed fearful, but a little pipistrelle bat was quite unperturbed as it hunted mosquitoes between the trees. As we watched the sky, a very large bird, possibly a heron, appeared at a great height. It seemed to be at loggerheads with baffling air currents and vanished suddenly sucked into a dark blue storm cloud. What was it doing at eagle-height, braving the mysteries of a storm?

Pictures in the Snow

Surlingham, February 13th, 1962

Tonight I stood for a little while down on the fen staithe watching snow play in diffused moonlight. Gusts from the north drove the feather specks of snow across the fen in strange shimmering curtains surging and blowing, scudding like spindrift of the sea and sometimes clouding the darkness of the woods beyond with silver-grey mist.

There were clots of snow foam on meadowsweet, the birds-nest crowns of tussock sedges and straggling brambles huddled on the banks, and paths were virginally bright except in the false shadows in the lee of every bush and tree, which stood out like inky holes and fissures in a moon landscape.

A great winter tide was welling over the dyke banks, turning marshes into lakes and spreading dark but lustrous stains across the snow alongshore. By day one does not catch an uninterrupted view of the delicate irregularities of a flood's edge, but in the gently luminous snowscape of this chill night the whole stealth of the advance was revealed to perfection.

The water crept forward like a living plasmodium or flowing lava. Lobes of it ran with the speed of quicksilver into coypu's footprints and linked chains of puddles until they became united. Dark streaks moved out like roots and fingers; crescent bays became far-winding inlets. Molehills at first lost in the general blanket of snow come to stand like igloos holding out against the advancing summer as thawing waters isolated their white peaks one by one.

A Tough Job, Reed Cutting

Surlingham, February 26th, 1962

Reed cutting is looked upon as one of the more romantic and picturesque rural occupations, and those engaged in it are slow to complain of any hardship involved. Rather they dwell upon the pleasures of gathering a harvest from the wilderness away from mechanisation and the bleakness of arable land in winter.

No doubt there is satisfaction in seeing a reward for one's labour in mounting stacks of golden reed bunches. There is some messing about in boats, another attraction, and there is the joy of planning one's own campaign.

All the same one has to be tough and forbearing to tackle this work as a regular thing for three months of the year. In the past week I have put in a few hours at it myself and discovered some of the occupational hazards. To begin with, reeds are flinty in texture. After grasping a few hundred swathes firmly while cutting the stalks with a sickle. I noticed a tingling of the skin on my hands rather like 'pins and needles', and this persisted for 24 hours.

Reeds are so abrasive that they even wear down the finger nails of those who handle them regularly. They also reduce jackets to tatters very quickly through the carrying of bundles. If a wind is blowing while cutting is in progress reed plumes have a habit of striking the face and eyes, causing much discomfort. Splintering stalks cut the hands inevitably every day.

Even the most experienced campaigners stumble into oozy pulk holes in the marshes from time to time and return home more or less water-logged after a heavy day of mowing and stumbling across rough, quaking ground with loads of bunched reeds. I am not greatly surprised that experienced reed cutters are scarce these days.

Dark Magic of the Fen

Surlingham, March 11th, 1962

Tonight a friend and I went off in a punt to enjoy the dark magic of the fen waterways for an hour or so. The night was strangely calm and cool with a small crescent moon peeping between high clouds.

For once there was hardly a sparkle on the waters; the Fen Channel lay like a sullen

stream of lead before us and the little broads were cloaked in the shadows and reflections of trees so that they became mere blanks of mysterious space out of which only near objects loomed up in procession as we moved forward.

We slipped past black hummocks of sedge and brushed black, snaky sallow boughs jutting out from the shores. Reeds, winter-pale, stood faintly glistening and ill-defined, merged with the dim, cloud-smudged skirts of the sky. The tremulous cry of a brown owl echoed across the valley and we heard the 'smee-oos' of widgeon gossiping in a hidden pool.

From time to time a wood pigeon or a moorhen would be startled out of a bush with crashing wings while loudly quacking mallard would resent our intrusion and rise heavily from the water ahead. One effect of the general obscurity was that for much of the time we were moving very slowly although I was using my one propelling oar vigorously enough. This was most noticeable when we were crossing the broads because we could not see the shores properly.

We achieved a sense of speed only towards the end of our journey when we travelled along a dyke through the woods and could look up at tall trees against the sky.

Golden Evening on the Broad

Surlingham, May 7th, 1962

We have just enjoyed a golden evening on Rockland Broad, idling with the swans and crested grebes. The tender green of young reed colts was beginning to assert itself here and there where the old culms remained to give shelter, but there were also forlorn, muddy bays and flats, jagged with black stumps of reeds which would never come to life again.

Pied lapwings and piping redshanks bobbed about in the oozy places, gorgeous shoveller drakes chased one another in the sky so fast that as they hurtled over us in circling, their pinions produced a drumming sound like that made by snipe.

The liquid notes of the cuckoos were mingled with the squabbling cries of gulls and clinking of coot. Sentinel herons stood like figures carved in ivory at intervals round the far sunlit shore; others flapped slowly over Surlingham Wood with a fleece of high golden clouds behind them, as though embroidered darkly on a beautiful Chinese screen.

The honey scent of willow catkins reached us in warm draughts of air from the fen and we saw bumble bees making long straight flights over the Broad as they went in quest of nectar and pollen.

On our way home by the Fen Channel we saw fish jumping everywhere, which showed that they had assembled as usual for May spawning. Towards sundown scores of swifts arrived to hawk gnats, and pipistrelle bats came out before they departed.

A Glow-worm's Toilet

Surlingham, April 13th, 1964

This morning I picked up a female glow-worm which was wandering over a patch of mossy turf in the garden. On taking a closer look at the flat, caterpillar-like insect, I noticed some traces of snail slime on a part of its body. It looked plump and well fed, so in all probability it had recently completed a meal of snail.

I decided to keep the glow-worm under observation for a few days, and for this purpose it was placed with some damp moss in a conical glass flask. Within a few minutes of having been introduced to its new abode, the creature began to perform an elaborate toilet. While legs gripped a tuft of moss and the head remained motionless, a round brush-like pad was extruded from the tail and used rather like a vacuum-cleaner on various parts of the body.

The pad, which was kept moistened by a special secretion, washed and brushed off particles of dirt and slime and, being perfectly flexible, it could be twirled about to reach every other portion of the glow-worm's body surface.

Under a strong lens I discovered that the tail-brush was in the form of a rosette of narrow finger-like processes, capable of swelling and shrinking like the tentacles of a polyp.

Later, when the insect began crawling again, I saw that the tail-pad had yet another function: it was used as an extra limb which enabled the glow-worm to climb up the inside of the glass flask for a short distance, by sticking to it where the claws could not get a grip.

Thoughts on the
Underground at Goldhawk Road

River of shining rails and lightning,
  Knobs on springs and green doors sliding,
Whistle and roar and a speed that's frightening,
  Black and yellow and white, hell-riding
Under a City's dust.

Goldhawk Road in a terrible gloaming,
  Veiled by a wreath of lights in mourning:
Stop for the grey, anonymous homing,
  Pause for the morrow's heart-beat warning
And the recurrent 'must!'

Oh, think of the fresh green frog that hops
  On a magic moor in the West,
And wild Welsh women that spin like tops
  On a purple mountain's crest.
Oh, think of the Gold Hawk in your dreams,
  And the country's wilder heart,
Where jaundiced journeys and mechanised screams
  Have no part
In what the jewelled day allows
  To children of the sun:
To birds a-wing and Man that ploughs
  Till his course be run.

Let Us Keep Our Serenity

Surlingham, April 22nd, 1964

'And this our life, exempt from public haunt,
    Finds tongues in trees, books in the running brooks,
Sermons in stones and good in everything.'
    'I would not change it.'

So Shakespeare in 'As You Like It' forestalled Gilbert White in presenting the gentle outlook of the country philosopher living close to nature. Now, 400 years after the poet's birth, the English countryside is vastly changed, yet in this thickly populated island miraculously there are still wildernesses 'exempt from public haunt'; where 'daisies pied and violets blue, and lady-smocks all silver-white, and cuckoo-buds of yellow hue do paint the meadows with delight,' and great green spaces where 'the lark at heaven's gate sings.'

Here in East Anglia we have largely escaped the stranglehold of industrial expansion and the sprawling over-growth of cities. But we have been reminded recently of what professional planners have in mind for the future; a more even distribution of industry, homes and people over the length and breadth of the land until ultimately it will become impossible to find a secluded wilderness.

No place will be 'exempt from public haunt'. With this threat in the offing I make no apology for standing out against it for what I believe to be the ultimate good.

I am very jealous for the pastoral peace of the East Anglian countryside. If it is destroyed, where will town-dwellers and all the sick-of-suburbs people turn to find unspoiled country? Let us remain a breathing space for the cure of souls rejoicing in honest agriculture, forestry and the like and cherishing the serene beauty of our Broads and coast. I am sure we can still do this and live.

Gold and Silver

Surlingham, October 11th, 1964

Autumn's gift of a gold and silver morning transfigured the fen scene when I went out just after breakfast today. The air was still and the sky blue and robins were singing thinly but sweetly in the trees, while pigeons cooed in sun-warmed ivy bowers and jays squabbled hoarsely in the sallow bushes.

The grasses and sedges were crisp underfoot where frost lingered in the shadows. The sword leaves of yellow flag iris were prickly with the ice crystals and nodding umbels of angelica looked as though they had been dipped in icing sugar. The reeds were nodding and dripping where the sun warmed them and melted drops of frost, water glittered like diamonds everywhere with an occasional dazzling flash of greater magnitude, almost blinding in intensity. Mist was smouldering and blue against the dark background of the woods and the bare mud of ditch banks on the sunny side was steaming furiously with the rapid absorption of radiance.

The sagging nets of spiders' webs festooned the vegetation, every thread silver-beaded. As I stood on the marsh a blue-tit dropped into a patch of reeds a few yards away and began to peck at the base of a sheathing leaf scattering dew drops in showers. Presently a passing crow disturbed the tit and it flew off. I finished prising open the reed sheath which it had been attacking so vigorously and inside I discovered three tiny shining brown beetles (*Olibrus corticalis*) snuggly hibernating in the cavity; they little knew how near they had been to disaster.

Charm of a Queen

Surlingham, November 26th, 1964

In summer, Barton Broad reflects blue skies and snowy-breasted clouds in her darkly silvered mirror; lilies ride the waves lapping her bays, and shores fringed with reed and gladdon sparkle with every tint of green and gold.

Today when I visited this queen of broads I found her in a very different mood; cool serene and remote from summer's gaieties. In the grey light of autumn the waters lay almost lifeless except where ripples of the wind created splashes of light far off across the long fairway. The crested grebes had gone to sea and cormorants with crow-black wings and snaky heads were fishing in their place, while gulls were dipping to the waters with the grace of fairy doves where in summer, swallows had peopled the air everywhere.

The shores seemed far away in their desolation, but still beautiful in their pastel hues of pale gold, russet and misty purple, with brush-wood fringing the horizon above the traceries of reed and sedge. Presently, approaching a little staithe at Catfield, I heard the tinkle of a bearded tit in the reeds and caught sight of a royal fern glowing like a fiery bush in a jungle, while a marsh harrier floated and flapped above a nearby sedge fen.

A Winter Picture

Surlingham, December 2nd, 1964

This afternoon I walked across the fen towards the river, from the valley's edge where crumpled silver leaves swathed the stalks of meadow-

sweet, to the reed beds standing in black ice. Along the path I noticed leafy rosettes of marsh thistles and ragged robin conspicuously green where most of summer's stalks and leaves lay in brown, bedraggled heaps about them.

Willows and sallows stood bare with brown besoms of twigs silhouetted against the sky. Scarlet berries hung yet in clusters on the guelder rose bushes, but they were crumpled soft and drooping and many of their pips had been scattered by fieldfares and blackbirds.

In some places the track was squelchy with black mud and in others crisp and crackling underfoot where the ice remained from a long freezing earlier in the week. Here and there I saw quantities of brown seeds of yellow flag spilled on the ground and some of them had been nibbled by small rodents. The sallow boughs were wreathed about with hops, now a rich rust colour, and lighter brown capsules of bellbine beloved by pheasants in winter.

Grey green lichens sodden with recent rain lay thick upon the twigs, where bluetits were busy hunting for tiny white scale insects. Redwings and fieldfares crossed my path erratically from time to time and I found almost the entire plumage of a blackbird newly plucked by a hawk in the middle of the path.

Arrived at a great reed bed, I stood still for ten minutes while bearded tits gathered all round me, some of them approaching within arm's reach as they hung on the reed plumes picking at the small fluffy seeds. Their soft plumage matched the pinkish hues of the reed tops and the orange gold of withering leaves and straw perfectly.

As they swung low on the fluffy plumes they kept up a family conversation in brief sweet notes which took the form of repeated phrases thus: 'Tee-tee-pretty, tit, tit, tit.' I noticed that whereas many other titmice commonly feed upside down the bearded tits usually attacked the reed heads in an upright position.

I enjoy the colours and patterns of gay frocks and furnishings, and the more demure tints and textures of buildings old and new. And when it comes to looking on the Face of Nature I can be thrilled to the core by the radiant beauty of flowers in the mass and singly, for sheer colour as well as for grace of form, and equally I am made happy by the quieter and more delicate tones and patterns of a winter landscape down to its smallest details.

Today I spent a pleasant hour on Hevingham Heath, one of the few large tracts of wild, undulating moorland held intact against the jealous advance of agriculture and forestry in this county.

Just now there is no blazing glory of gorse or rainbow brilliance of heather but the sere, rushy places are richly embroidered with a fantastic array of bog mosses, green and fresh with winter's moisture.

Peaty paths which were adorned by blue gentians in autumn are now carpeted with curious algae and creeping liverworts. Where the black soil is encrusted by swarms of beautiful lichens with their filigrees of silver threads, grey-green goblets and knobs of scarlet wax.

The bracken, erect, tousled or flattened, is of every shade of russet, old brick and sunset pink. The heath is like a tapestry woven by the fairies of its underworld from the threads of its struggling life.

In winter, as in summer, the embroidering continues. I find it strange that so few eyes look upon this wonder for their soul's delight.

An Unspoilt Haven

Surlingham, March 6th, 1967

This afternoon I visited a desolate little harbour on the North Norfolk coast, where the final loops of the Stiffkey river converge and gush through a sluice into a broad, deep creek and sweep out into the sea.

To reach this little-known point I followed a farm track from the coast road west of Morston, where undulating ploughland adjoins the green meadows of Stiffkey 'freshes'. This land must have experienced a turbulent history, judging from the quantity of angular pebble mixed with its loam, and by the fact that in places the top soil has been scoured down to the underlying chalk and capped to seaward with bluffs of rounded pebbles during one of the later interludes between ice ages.

In the harbour, where stalwart mussel boats keeled over at low tide, I found the thickest accumulation of salt marsh litter I had ever seen. Apparently the prevailing set of both tide and wind had combined to heap layer after layer of dead grassy material along one stretch of the shore. The material resembled long weathered hay, and must have been a yard thick in places, almost burying the tall bushes of shrubby sea-blite growing there.

From the shore I found myself looking out to the top of Blakeney Point, with its sands gently luminous in the sunshine. Twenty Brent geese rose from the water, looking as black as cormorants silhouetted against the gold of the distant sands.

I was happy to come upon this out of the way haunt of fishermen and wildfowl still free from the press of holidaycraft and commercial exploitation.

Flying over the Broads

Surlingham, April 26th, 1967

Early this evening a friend took me for an exploratory flight over the whole of the Broads district in a light aeroplane. I can think of no more delightful experience, especially at this season when spring sunshine reveals the beauty of sprouting verdure in fields, woods and marshes and at the same time shows the backcloth of winter's faded vegetation and clear waterways.

First we followed the Waveney's slender silver thread with its horseshoe curves and loops from Bungay to Beccles, glowing with a russet warmth on its hill. There were willow shaded reaches and others winding for miles through bice green meadows.

From the alder carrs of Aldeby we crossed a wide expanse of dyke land to find Barnby Broad shining like a brown eye in the middle of a wood. Then Oulton Broad lay lead-blue beneath us, with its scatter of brightly painted boats and great golden swidge of reed beds matching the colour of Scroby's little island of sand, which we could see off distant Yarmouth.

Presently we swung away to savour the enchantment of Fritton's forest-bordered lake and the jewelled chain of the Lound ponds stretching almost to the sea behind it. Then over to the white walls of Burgh Castle, standing sentinel at the head of Breydon and the great estuary itself.

A vast level stretch of grazing marshes held our gaze as we flew on towards Acle and the North River, and we saw that the old natural salt marsh creeks could still be detected in root-like patterns on which an artificial drainage system had been imposed.

Flying over Broadland—II

Surlingham, April 27th, 1967

We crossed the Bure near Stokesby, where a glittering, sinuous Muckfleet led us to the lovely fingered broads of Flegg. Round Burgh Broad we were puzzled by the minutely cracked appearance of large tracts of brown reed-swamp and fen, and wondered if old coypu tracks might have created the mysterious patterns visible from the air.

At Horsey, we saw a cloudy sediment fanning out from the mouth of Waxham Cut into the clear depths of the Mere, and presently we were able to trace this to the numerous tributary ditches in arable land near Palling, where the seeping water was rust-red with iron bacteria. Swinging round over Hickling, we were surprised to see a milkiness in the main channel all the way across the broad.

At Upton Broad, a brown pool nestling in the heart of a jungle of trees, we espied a kingfisher, just visible a thousand feet below as a minute flashing speck of blue, like some jewelled insect, moving with steady purpose across the dark waters. At Ranworth Broad we could see white spots dotted about some rafts moored at one end, and these were probably terns newly returned to nest there.

Passing up the Bure valley, we crossed the afforested heathlands of Horstead and Fel-thorpe and found ourselves looking down on a spectacular series of gravel-pit lakes along the Wensum, while many newer gravel workings in the district were a highly conspicuous feature of the landscape, giving promise of new pools in the not very distant future.

Then, leaving Norwich in a dreamy haze, we followed the Yare to the bright oasis of Surlingham and Rockland Broads, where we bid the swans goodnight and swung away to land at Seething.

The Hurry

If I'd my way, 'twould be to stay
    And sniff at all the roses
In gardens where they seem to stare
    And pine for pretty noses.

I dare not sigh, the minutes fly;
    The dusty pavement claims me;
And yet I yearn to finger fern
    While duty blinds and lames me.

The office and the queueing stand,
    The strict demands of dinner,
News bulletins and salvage bins
Ensnare me for a sinner

On Sunday, when I drop my pen,
    'Tis but to take a shovel
And earth the leeks or feed the beaks
    Behind my six-roomed hovel.

So, like the sun, I snatch my fun
    In little dew-point flashes;
I touch and go, like harassed snow:
    A thing of dots and dashes.

Yet when I think that bees don't blink,
    I'm rather more contented,
And after all, a human thrall
    Is only half invented.

Written at a bus stop, 1943

Enchanted Woods

Surlingham, February 14th, 1968

This evening the tremulous, querulous music of wood owls drew me out of doors to sample the magic and mystery of a wilderness bathed in the light of a full moon.

From the edge of the fen where tall feather-topped reeds swayed in a wintry breeze I stared at a dappled cloudland through witch-broom tops of pollard willows. Beside me an ivy-mantled oak stood like a rugged giant with its head towering into outer space, but I enjoyed an intimate view of its elbowed boughs and knotty buds silhouetted against the moon's silver screen.

I visited a lone pine and passed through the gloom of its noble shadow, where densely-needled boughs wreathed the trunk like lowering thunder clouds. Then wandering through a woodland glade I found myself in a fairy forest of silver birch wands, pollarded beeches and dappled leafy ways. Seen in shadow, lambstail catkins on hazel sprigs appeared to be fashioned of black velvet, while beech cupules looked furry where they were still attached within the ranks of slender pointed buds.

Here and there lights flashed from glossy ivy leaves trembling in the breeze. There were faint cracklings and whisperings of brittle twigs and leaves, and evergreens rustled like swishing silken skirts from time to time.

There are no werewolves in our enchanted woods, yet these haunts of peace and beauty are avoided at night by those people still held enthralled by primitive instincts.

The Woods Bewitched

Surlingham, May 24th, 1967

This evening the woods were bewitched by the gayest spirits of spring. A rainbow towered in a leaden sky to the east; a chorus of birds filled the leafy aisles with music, rain fell in golden drops like a curtain in a transformation scene,

while the setting sun glowed like a great fire in the west.

Rhododendron blossoms took on a brighter blush, cresting the spidery patchwork of greenery with vivid colour. Robins eluded the raindrops as they swooped beneath dark evergreens, snatching at midges. Gold-green oaks and queenly birches trembled almost imperceptibly in the evening breeze.

The last pale stars of poet's narcissus nodded in a throng of bluebells tinged with amethyst translucence by the declining sun. A lordly pheasant strolled across a glade and slipped into the shadows. A tuneful cuckoo burst upon the scene almost giddily after a long silence. And in the green world new and refreshed by rain every detail of leafy tracery was revealed by a strange light; the curled fronds of young ferns, the arching brambles, the raindrop-beaded spears of grass twining honeysuckle and blossoming may with pale pillars of trees supporting a vast filigree of foliage like the roof of a temple hallowed by the peace of Eden.

As the Sun went down

Surlingham, October 22, 1967

As the sun went down this afternoon it left no trail of fiery splendour, but the gold of it shone on the poplars and a faint crystallisation of haze above the marshscape here became suffused with the merest blush betwixt brown reed plumes and a frosty zenith. The air was still and cold, yet as daylight faded columns of dancing gnats rose from the grass almost to the height of the tallest trees.

I watched them in their frenzied ecstasy following their movements individually with ease against the pallor of the sky as they rose and sank like giddy water fleas in an aquarium. Theirs were by no means the only silhouettes overhead. While I stood on watch at the edge of the fen I saw other insects flying on straight courses in various directions, some between trees and others towards the sun's clear afterglow, each on some mission known only to itself.

At higher elevations great chevrons of gulls and untidy gaggles of mixed jackdaws and rooks travelled towards the east. Jays flapped low across the marsh from one cover to another. Blackbirds sped to their roosts with tails cocked as they made a final swoop into hiding. Wild duck moved off at speed like miniature jet planes. A pheasant crowed and skimmed the reeds like a bolt from a cannon before it crashed into the undergrowth and was lost.

And finally, as the dancing gants sank into the shadows fieldfares arrived in noisy haste swerving this way and that as they made for the shelter of the fen wilderness.

Glory of the Oak

Surlingham, May 15th, 1968

It must have been in a spring like this that Chaucer was moved to describe the oaks as 'gladde bright green.' At this moment, just as May blossoms are bursting in the hedges and tall cow parsley is at the height of its lacy flowering, oaks are the chief glory of the woods.

Their young leaves, some of them crimped and curled and others spreading daintily like gold-green petalled stars, hang in brave candelabra, bosses and cascades, catching the sunlight and transmuting it into every tint of green and bronze.

The ancient oak woods of England were the backbone of her strength, yielding a wealth of timber for the building of houses and ships, firing for the hearths, charcoal for smelting, bark for tanning and acorns for pigs. The beauty and the poetry of their renewal of growth every spring meant much to all who dwelt within sight of them; they were noble spirits in the land.

Today they occupy only a very small part of their former kingdom, and alien conifers have taken over most of their latter-day strongholds quite recently, to the sorrow of those of us who cherish oak woods not only for their trees but also for their centuries-old carpets of bluebells, orchids, primroses, wild lilies and other delightful flowers which are doomed to perish in the gloom of fir plantations.

However, no doubt we shall still have a good sprinkling of park oaks gracing the stately homes of East Anglia for many years to come.

Life and Colour

Surlingham, June 9th, 1968

This has been a day of lighthearted, high-flying, twitching swallows, blue skies and balmy breezes. Cuckoos have been assiduously tuneful and chaffinches in the treetops have been practising their wheezy, tumbling cadences hour after hour.

This afternoon our heather purple rhododendrons, now in their glory, and contrasting vividly with the green of young bracken, and the gold sprays of broom, attracted legions of insects on the sunny side. The visitors included peacock, large white and brimstone butterflies, occasional queen wasps and a great many huge and heavy queen bumblebees which became thickly dusted with pollen. I did not see many hive bees in the throng.

Near by, in a sun-dappled glade, I saw a pale green lacewing fly travelling backwards in a curiously ungainly fashion, threshing the air slowly with its long wings rather like a helicopter about to land in a circumscribed jungle clearance.

Where the sun beat down on the bracken small brown wasps with dark and silver lines on their wings emerged to flutter around briefly, and then settle where they looked rather like fallen petals lodged casually on the green fronds.

In one lush, grassy spot I found an all-scarlet cardinal beetle climbing a hogweed stalk, while wall-brown butterflies sipped at the chalices of buttercups a few feet away, and under the oaks the ground was littered with ruby red currant galls, newly fallen with the discarded catkins on which they had developed during the spring.

There was life and colour in every niche and cranny of the undergrowth, and at every step one breathed some new fragrance of earth and greenery and flowers distilled in the gentle air of June.

Cliff Plant Variety

Surlingham, July 16th, 1968

The majestic cliffs between Cromer and Mundesley, notorious for their land-slips, provide a wide variety of habitats for plants, albeit unstable ones.

As towering bluffs of glacial sands, loams and clays slide and topple beachward, mainly through the action of under-cutting springs, many different constituent materials are exposed. Eroding current-bedded sands, long leached by rain, offer a welcome to weeds of acid soils such as sheep's sorrel and corn marigold, while the sludge of the more clayey glacial 'till' supports lush growths of coltsfoot.

Well-drained slopes of mixed loam and sand are colonised in some places by magnificent brambles, and lower down within the influence of salt spray, sea buckthorn flourishes in beautiful grey-green thickets.

Lime from finely comminuted shells and chalk abounds in some sections of the cliffs and is responsible for the presence of crisp carline thistles, bowers of old man's beard and clumps of yellow kidney vetch. Small rare trefoils creep in the sandy turf and fragrant pink centauries spring from sand-sprinkled chalk wash.

One can come across anything from a bee orchid to a crowberry at home in some favoured niche of this ever-changing face of the crumbling mountain of spoil of half a million years of geological stockpiling.

Airborne seeds, like insects, tend to be wafted down at the high cliff edge in very large numbers. The coast is also a reception area for a great many bird migrants, some of them transporting seeds from far afield. It is therefore hardly surprising that the cliff wilderness is composed of such a rich flora.

And because of the active erosion taking place, no one type of vegetation can ever dominate the scene permanently at any point.

Brink of Winter

Surlingham, November 10th, 1968

The fog-bound woods were adrip and disturbed by the patter of falling acorns this morning as I tramped with swishing steps through the litter of russet leaves and sought the peace of the open fen.

Presently, standing by a dyke, I watched the pale orb of the sun emerging from the mist. At first it was like a moon face in a grey world. Brown pinnacles of reeds appeared in silhouette against it like a rabble of aged and haggard travellers bowed down with weariness in the dawn of a hopeless day; but minute by minute the scene brightened in a triumph of silvery diffusion.

With frost-blue spears of sedge at my feet and the freckled gold of sallows looming out of the distant haze. I listened to the chortlings of fieldfares feasting on guelder rose berries while from time to time a cock pheasant would utter a volley of 'alarums' which reverberated like gunfire.

In a thicket of bleached crooked wands, gossamer hung in frail nets and fairy hammocks. Then an urgent wren whirred into the midst of this trembling tracery and scattered dewdrops in all directions as it peered and poked about for its breakfast.

As the mist thinned and became more luminous, blackbirds came swooping to the berried bushes and elfin bluetits and baby-faced long-tailed tits made haste to go their rounds of the sallow bushes and spider-laden herbs of the fen. But I think the robins must have breakfasted early because I now heard them singing a welcome to the sun piercingly sweet and cheering on this brink-of-winter morning.

Dawn of a new day

Surlingham, June 21st, 1970

Either the warmth of the night or the loud pealing of a thrush's notes woke me at three o'clock in time to set forth into the fragrance and mystery of a midsummer dawn. Moon daisies shone in the tall grass, though dewy clover leaves were still folded in sleep.

The air was filled with gossamer and mosquitos zoomed at me from every quarter. Glow worm lamps had faded, and a white ground mist lay over the fen, with spikes of iris and flowering grasses pricking through it in silhouette. Small bats whisked round the trees in a final spurt of excitement before retiring to their crevices and they dived at me like the angry terns of Blakeney, squeaking explosively in my face for a fraction of a second.

While the bird chorus rose to a crescendo in the nearby woods, and shrilling wrens whirred out of the undergrowth, sedge-warblers churred and chattered in the reeds, and first one and, presently, three cuckoos began calling. One was in perfect tune, the second doubled its lower note and the third was sadly flat and faltering.

A cock crowed up in the village, but there were no echoes from pheasants at their roosts just then, although I could hear some conversational greylags stirring on the broad. Strangely enough, song thrushes dominated the woodland chorus, while the half light lingered, and it was not until ten minutes past four that the first blackbird joined in (by no means ecstatically) and it was then, also, that I heard the first bumble bee buzzing round a patch of comfrey.

Colour flooded back gently into flowers everywhere now; the yellow irises in the fen, pink ragged robin, valerian and dog rose and lordly foxgloves, half in woodland shade. The last pale moths zigzagged into hiding and another golden day had arrived.

Threshold to Elysian Fields

Surlingham, April 6th, 1971

Our country churchyards have become increasingly precious as little havens of wildlife. In some districts they are the only remaining refuges of gentle slow-worms and very often they contain relics of an ancient woodland flora which has long since vanished from the surrounding countryside. Their funereal yews and ivied walls provide nesting places for song birds.

As generations come and go, memories in stone pass gently into Nature's embrace where the velvet of mosses and the gold and silver tracery of lichens spreads over the crumbling rock-slabs of the tombs. For centuries churchyards have been hallowed places of beauty and contemplation where poets lingered and sorrows were healed with the coming of spring.

Like the urned chambers of tumuli which are still landmarks on some of our heaths and fields, even indeed like that great monument of funereal magnificence clustered in the Valley of the Kings, our 'God's Acres' are a threshold of eternity in the symbolism of our people and it is there that Nature draws us back into the Garden of Eden.

However, a hoary, rambling churchyard is regarded with distaste by some tidy-minded members of the community and some ser-

Norwich to London by Rail

Zump and clicker, gathering roar:
   A drummed and fleeing pulse of sound
As chequered fields and treescapes slide away.
   Queen Ann gable, black-fanged oak;
Pied cattle, stolid on their plots of green;
   A drift of gulls, like pearls
Strewing dark ploughland;
   Forgotton hollows, bright with pools and reeds
And wild duck unafraid.
   No sailor ever sped the seas like this,
Nor babbling stream so swiftly ran its course.
   The sky itself is left behind
In a long drift of clouds and circling birds.
   A lone pine leaps a hill;
A silver brush of birches closes in;
   Huddles of mossy pantiles tilt the light
In the warm beauty of a village street.
   But now my shuttle plunges into grief:
A suburb's craziness of junk and boxy homes:
   A graveyard of fair dreams;
A toyland smiling through its tears;
   An Eden in the bonds of guilt and greed.
But Nature is not quelled
   And bracken, buddleja and feverfew
Are perched like sprites
   On Liverpool Street's dark walls,
Where Time is stilled and born again
   In the twilight of a journey's end.

(1972)

Mousehold Glories

Surlingham, September 8th, 1971

vants of the church and perhaps most particularly by municipal officials to whom the care of graveyards falls from time to time. Then, in the interests of convenience headstones are removed to boundaries (or dumped) and grave mounds are levelled so that a mown lawn is created, after the fashion of a bowling green or football pitch.

Similarly, every little weed is ousted from masonry and even the flagged or gravelled paths are kept 'decent' by the use of weed-killers. I find the more extreme among these practices very saddening at a time when, with only a minimum of management such as a brief hay-making each summer, village churchyards could be cherished as much for their richness of living beauty as for their reminder of our passing into the Elysian fields.

This afternoon I savoured the immemorial beauty of Mousehold Heath, where the fragrance of sun-warmed heather and dwarf autumnal gorse on the hills rose about me and I looked towards the city—a radiant colourful nest of buildings still dominated as of old by Cathedral spire and Castle keep.

I strolled down gulleys through the birch woods, where again the air was sweet with the scent of leaf mould and moss, and groups of early toadstools here and there. There were touches of autumn gold in the trees, and in places drifts of tiny birch seeds which, when spread on the palm of my hand, looked like miniature flying doves.

The more open glades were fringed by tall hawkweeds topped with shaggy yellow blossom, and there were damp spots moistened no

doubt by feeble springs where urn-mosses formed lush carpets despite the scorching weather of the past few days.

I saw very few butterflies, but there were a few dappled greylings on the open heathland and an occasional small tortoiseshell gliding by the roadside.

I caught a glimpse of Mousehold's remarkable double-flowered brambles in one grassy place where they have flourished for as long as I can remember. I know of no other wild colony of these rose pink beauties which produce only their freakish blossoms and never any berries.

The heath is not so open or so far flung as it was in the days of Crome and Cotman and George Borrow, but it is still a glorious vantage point for the contemplation of immortal things and for renewing faith in life.

Glory of Breckland

February, 1972

This morning I enjoyed the peace of Thetford Forest as a traveller along its almost deserted roads on the fringe of a battle training area, which was also utterly quiet. The sun shone on red pine-boles and warmed the long, straight rides with their straw-gold turf and russet bracken.

Along my devious route the country opened up here and there to expose far vistas of the old breck with sheep grazing, flints strewing the tracks and clumps of thorn, elder and birch adding beauty to the scene. I also caught glimpses of some of the old Scots pine belts planted as windbreaks long ago.

Lovers of wild, windswept country felt some sadness at the prospect of widespread afforestation back in the 1920's, but the new beauty which has been created not only still retains much of the old; it has brought the ancient magic of forest life into a desert, so that we now have a wealth of woodland birds, more squirrels, wandering deer and even more butterflies of certain kinds flourishing in a paradise of their liking.

Instead of an endless gloom of conifer plantations there is endless variety of pattern. The younger stands of trees cast a deep shade, it is true, but the thinning of poles at successive stages lets in more and more light and as the older trees come to perfection, they are indeed lovely to behold. There are also a great many screens of deciduous trees, no longer mere palisades of young growth, but with the arching grace of maturity and dappled spaces in between.

Over the years I have discovered that the foresters of our time, like their predecessors, are imbued with a great love of the trees they tend and the rich and varied wildlife about them. In its transformation Breckland has achieved a perfection far greater than was dreamt of when the change was initiated fifty years ago. It has become one of East Anglia's greatest glories.

Awakening of April

1972

This has been a day of contrasts, with black squalls of rain and hail sweeping across the valley, majestic cloudscapes creating dark blue distances beyond the sun-gold of reed-beds and glitter of wet, green sedges and willow catkins; chill winds ruffling the waters off and on, at times a glow of warmth and peace, with wildfowl dozing in the bays.

The wakening of April has begun to coax life from the winter-brown marshes very swiftly in the past week, and even reluctant reed-colts are now shooting up like smooth asparagus in the stubbles, surrounded by the splendour of marsh marigolds. Early willows, like hazels in the woods, display the tender green of young leaves. In shadowy swamps there are verdant clumps of water forget-me-nots, neat, blue-green tufts of sedge and the lengthening sword leaves of irises. Nettles have sprouted in the jungles and already, small tortoiseshell butterflies have been laying eggs on their young foliage.

This evening I watched several shelduck flying over our broad, strictly in pairs and conversing with the gentleness of lovers in whistling tones very different from the strident cackles uttered earlier in the mating season. Bunches of teal rose and circled in evening flight, at times towering to a considerable height, so that their quick whistlings became a silvery twitter overhead. Although they had joined forces in this ritual exercise, I could still detect that each flock was formed of couples peeling off fraternally as the circling skeins spread out from time to time. Presently I caught a brief glimpse of a small blue hawk, undoubtedly a merlin still active on the scene of its winter's hunting.

Spring's Sylvan Beauty

May 31st, 1972

Today's showers and strong winds died away toward sundown, and when I took an evening stroll through the woods, paths were flooded with ruddy gold, while dappled light played about the snaky upper branches of trees and the bowers of dancing, twinkling leaves.

Looking up through chinks in the greenery I could see swifts arching in a blue sky. Numbers of small caterpillars of the green tortrix moth were dangling on threads from the oaks at various levels, rather as though they might have been destined to float away on the first breath of wind.

The wood was filled with bird music, with wrens, robins and small warblers trilling fitfully, a song thrush calling like a curlew and a blackbird fluting like a golden oriole. Bluebells had finished flowering under the beeches and bracken was growing tall, with only a few of the young fronds yet unfurled.

Long shadows streaked across mossy knolls and the spangled leaf-carpet, which was littered with many fresh green leaves and shoots, wind-stripped from the trees a little earlier. As I looked down the aisles of sylvan beauty, silver birches were illumined by the evening sun and rhododendrons glowed in rosy splendour, tier above tier on great mounds of leafiness looming out of the shadows.

November Delights

November 2nd, 1972

Grey November has its special delights for those of us who are fortunate to live in the country. As mist disperses slowly in the mornings, hedgerows spring into sharp relief, with spoky umbels of hogweed, withered nettle spikes and ragged, arching brambles looming up larger than life.

While wayside herbs make stiffly graceful friezes in silhouette, the banks and verges glow with the richest colours of the year as leaves turn crimson, purple and every tint of gold, while scarlet rose-hips, trailing wreaths of bryony and clustered berries on the hawthorns shine, jewel-bright, with morning dew.

Roads are littered with pools of dead leaves shed by overhanging trees in the still of the night, those from the ash still green as in life, contrasting with the orange of sycamore, russet of elm and oak and the pastel yellows of various others.

Everywhere, trees attain the dignity of age as bare twigs come into view in their thinning crowns and summer's cloak of glory is shed. At this time, when wispy leaves drift down like butterflies, one is aware of the living spirit of the trees as much as in spring when buds are swelling to burgeon anew with greenery and flowers.

Now, also we find ourselves invigorated by a

keenness in the air which sharpens the senses. In the mists of November nights a spicy fragrance is distilled. Sometimes, especially when the first gleam of morning sunshine breaks through and pheasants crow in welcome, the air seems to be heavy with scent like that which pervades churches on harvest festival Sundays. It is as though the wine of the year has ripened and overflowed from the cask.

Insects' Golden Hour

June 2nd, 1973

When beams of sunlight shine between trees towards sunset, especially in calm weather, one can watch the flight of many small insects which seem to have wings of gold glittering against the dark background of foliage and shadows.

There are gnats dancing rhythmically, getting higher and higher until they form dark swarms above the treetops. Smaller midges keep to lower levels, shimmering sometimes in closely packed clouds and then dispersing suddenly as though by magic.

Other flies and flying beetles dart about in all directions, often at a remarkable speed, while fairy-like lacewings flutter and swoop awkwardly for short distances from time to time.

The sunbeams also pick out threads of gossamer in the air, spun by young spiders which use them as parachutes.

At this time of the year, in warm weather, small caterpillars often launch themselves on threads of silk in the same way and can drift to considerable heights, wafted upwards by warm air.

One evening recently I watched a spotted flycatcher swooping between the trees to snap at the larger insects as they came into view, and once a swallow dashed into the glittering throng, causing a brief disturbance.

When the light is low it is possible to see the airy world peopled with insects more clearly than at any other time and even to observe precisely the flurry caused by an intruding bird. Rather surprisingly, the insects break rank only for a few seconds and quickly resume their original formations. But if a mist begins to gather or a draught of cold air springs up, the tiny fliers retire from the scene in haste. They know by instinct when their golden hour is over.

Will-o'-the-Wisp World

November 22nd, 1973

In the moonlight tonight, weeping willows had silver tresses. Fallen leaves on paths formed bright mosaics and the rust and yellow of sycamore and beech foliage gleamed from the shadowy interlacing of hedges. Moisture had gathered here and there, reflecting the moonbeams in diamond points, small spots and crinkled blotches. Although there was no mist, the very brightness of the reigning orb created a will-o'-the-wisp world of dancing leaves and shifting shadows.

At this season, more than any other, if the night air is damp and mild, one meets with real lumonosity in lanes and woods. The mycelium of honey-tuft fungus sheets rotten tree trunks in ghostly greenish-white, revealed where loosened bark has come away. As dead leaves are disturbed underfoot, the vivid phosphorescence of certain centipedes is spilled and scattered as the creatures take fright.

No adult glow-worms are present in autumn, but their larvae shine in the dark, not pulsing nuptial signals as in June, but perhaps exercising their phosphorescent glow for some other purpose, such as exciting the curiosity of wandering molluscs intended as prey.

The Norfolk Wherry

Like a heap of bones where the elephants die
   Somewhere the wherrymen's quants must lie.
Where marsh mists creep o'er Hobrough's Yard.
   Old wherry masters post the guard
For the hulks of ships and the hulks of men
   Are wont to drift together again.
Once through the realms of reed and willow,
   Where otters snoozed on a sedgy pillow,
And midges danced in a summer sky
   To the bittern's boom and the peewit's cry
And a thousand larks all carolling high.
   Great sails swung in the day's sweet hours
By old green banks and wildling flowers
   Then as you sighted a skimming swallow,
A wherry soon would gently follow;
   But now you can take white wings all the way,
By the same lush swards and wild flowers gay.
   While dragonflies dart and whirligigs play.
And across your wake there'll come no sound
   Of wherryman's hail or joke profound:
For dusk has come at the end of this day,
   And there's mist where his craft of the water-path lay.
To tarry, slithery half-drowned shacks
   Come spars and tackle to rot in stacks;
And rats squeak foul riparian tattle
   O'er mouldering sheets that once gave battle
To Jolly Roger on the ramp;
   And if you venture with a lamp
Under the arches of tackle tangle –
   Of splintered spars and blocks that jangle—
You'll find old sails that are patched no more:
   For this is Forgotten Glory Store.

(1946)

(The association of the late Mr J S Hobrough with the passing of the Norfolk Wherry has been closer than that of any other man. Sooner or later most of them made a last voyage to his yard at Whitlingham to be broken up, and I know that he regretted their fate as much as anyone. Now that he has gone I would like to dedicate these few verses to his memory.)

The Wizardry of Frost

Surlingham, January 1st, 1974

The last golden day of the Old Year has been succeeded by the lavish silvering of frost begot of a mist which hung in the air all through today. Although the sun was visible for hours, it could not dispel the all-pervading chill.

Molehills remained hard frozen, like the road puddles, while ice gathered strength and opaqueness in pools and ditches. Leafless trees became hoary with white spicules which grew from the first sugar-like powdering overnight. Many twigs acquired a shaggy appearance, while delicate traceries based on wefts of gossamer festooned ivy bowers and hedgerows.

Frost patterns evolving on prickly gorse sprigs came to resemble greatly magnified snowflakes, with symmetrical starry forms. All green blades of grass, down curved with the weight of frosty encrustation, appeared furry with ermine such as Cinderella's Fairy Godmother might have created with the whisk of a wand. And there were feathery tops of some withered bent-grasses transformed into fantastic heaps of silver-threaded lace.

I came upon bramble leaves; plum purple, maroon, streaked with crimson and scarlet like the cheeks of ripe pippins, and all of them fringed and sprinkled with crystal brightness, while the prickles on their stalks were thickened and star-tipped.

Holly leaves were rimmed with white and their spines had grown long points of ice like the prickles of a porcupine. Tall thistles, burdocks and teasels were like ice warriors of the plant world, bristling with bright daggers from top to toe. Even the smooth reeds were clothed in snowy whiskers.

Such perfection in the wizardry of frost can only be achieved on a very still winter's day which allows the tiny spicules to gather and grow without disturbance.

Night Noises

Surlingham, April 1st, 1974

Even at night one can feel something of the magic of spring just now. When the sky remains clear after sundown there is soon a chill in the air, but this seems to distil the fragrances of mossy earth, grass, pine needles, sallow bloom and various tender herbs in the hedgerows as night mists gather.

Recently I took a walk in starlight with a tip-tilted half moon hanging in the western sky. A field pond was steaming like a witches' cauldron as mist was generated from its vapours. There was enough light in the sky to throw black, snaky shadows on trees across the road, and I could even see wayside gorse blossoms looking as pale as the moon itself.

There was perfect calm, with long periods of absolute silence, in this Broadland valley; but if one listened carefully, small night noises could be detected from time to time, such as the brief utterances of wild ducks and moorhens on the waterways, the mooing of coypus in the swamps and the caterwauling of owls. At one point I was momentarily startled by a wood mouse leaping and racing over the road, and I am sure I heard a hedgehog snuffling in the undergrowth.

Strangely enough I neither saw nor heard anything of the rabbits which frequent the area in fairly large numbers. It may be that they venture forth to feed and play mainly at dusk and dawn, and retire to their holes when the night's breath seems about to congeal into a frost.

Glory down by the River

Surlingham, May 26th, 1974

I followed an angler's path a little way along the River Tas the other day and came to a spot such as Shakespeare might have pictured when he set the scene for poor Ophelia's exit. There were great gnarled willows, dark alders and poplars, with thick nests of mistletoes in their crowns. Forests of hemlock and tall nettles with here and there a huge burdock covering much of the ground.

Suddenly I came to a bend in the stream and was astonished by the wealth of flowers clustered at the water's edge. There were vast masses of comfreys with drooping blossoms, every shade of heather, purple, pink and blue. These were interspered with luxuriant dame's violets, some white and others lilac, sheets of red campion, a glowing magenta, some smaller white flowers of garlic mustard, and many shining yellow patches of winter-cress. This rainbow ribbon of colour was reflected in the

Surlingham, May 30th, 1974

water, itself sparkling and providing glimpses of translucent water-lily leaves in the depth.

I had never seen such a glorious stretch of riverside in spring, nor quite the same assortment of wild flowers sharing a riparian site. The Tas valley is full of surprises and provides many beautiful vistas along its relatively short course before it joins the Yare at Norwich. Its hillside woods, marshy commons and homesteads, like the stream itself, have so far managed to retain something of the magic of a less urgent, less sophisticated time.

In the wood here this morning I stood for a while listening to the restless fluting of two cock golden orioles, as elusive and compelling as pan-pipes in their leafy maze. They had a challenging effect on other birds and both a song thrush and a blackbird gave superb performances nearby.

Tall oaks and birches gleaming where the sunshine touched their fresh young foliage, had the appearance of being infested with small caterpillars. Leaves silhouetted against the sky could be seen to have indented and

snipped edges and many had only the stalks left. Starlings were going the rounds of the tree tops, in family parties apparently, craking wheezily as they snatched at the caterpillars with the boisterousness and zest of rugby players in a scrum.

While these kept mainly to the oaks, smaller birds were busy collecting caterpillars from the smaller birch leaves. I saw great tits, willow warblers, a blackcap and two redpolls feasting in this way close to where I was standing. In all cases they tended to move from tree to tree fairly quickly, rather as though they meant to leave something for later visits.

Some of the young bracken fronds in the wood were already shoulder-high, but still of a tender gold-green hue and not creating much shade over the fading bluebells. I saw a large white butterfly flitting high about the crowns of the oaks, rather as though it was lost in the wood and was not quite sure whether to try and escape over the top or to amble on hopefully between the trees.

Presently a smaller (green-veined) white rose from a bramble patch and joined its larger relative. For a minute or two they tumbled together in the tree-tops, but finally decided that they were not a match and went their individual ways. I quite expected some insectivorous bird would make a sortie in their direction, but it seems caterpillars were the set dish for the day.

All on a June day

Surlingham, June 13th, 1974

Today's sunshine coaxed forth a delicious fragrance from trees, grass and wild flowers everywhere, as I remember the sweetness of hayfields in midsummer in the dreamy days of my youth. In the woods here, rosy rhododendrons are massed as richly as on their native hills far away; the bracken's mossy greenness is matched by the half-translucent verdure of oak, ash and birch leaves arched overhead.

In a sunlit glade towards the end of this afternoon, I saw my first red admiral butterfly of the summer, settled with wings outstretched on a bramble. Blackcaps were singing in silvery bursts from nearby trees and bushes, wrens

were popping about in all directions, thrushes were still in full song and young, speckled robins were snapping at flies along the paths.

Down on the fen this evening I stood in a peaceful corner sheltered from the cool but gentle breeze and looked out on the troops of yellow flags and white flat-topped flower heads of guelder rose which emitted a sweet and heady scent. Here and there a pink spike of spotted orchid blossom showed itself amongst grasses, buttercups and fading Lady's smocks and there were drifts of magenta pink ragged robin along some of the tracks.

Numerous swifts were patrolling the sky high over the woods and marshes, taking toll of a rise of shimmering insects from the sun-warmed countryside. A flock of a dozen lapwings passed up river, doubtless on the move on the completion of their nesting season in some distant area, although earlier today I found some of these birds still skirling and swooping anxiously where it was clear they had a young family to protect on a fenland field in Cambridgeshire.

Towards sunset, pipistrelle bats emerged to take their fill of gnats alongside the wood, just as goldswift moths began their erratic dances low over the fen vegetation, while a woodcock went hurtling by on a late 'roding' light, uttering its deep rattling croak as loudly as in the early days of spring courtship.

Sylvan Ballet

Surlingham, July 31st, 1974

This morning I happened to be looking at a very peaceful riverside scene when a wind sprang up quite suddenly and set the boughs of willow trees dancing and swinging. Pale green and silver green, the ribbon-leaves rippled and flowed, sometimes pawing the air as they were tossed high like the manes of rearing horses, only to be arrested in their wild bid for freedom by the restraining sinews of trunk and bough.

Sometimes they shuddered as a backdraught reversed the strain, rather as sails flutter just before a jibe. Here and there a slender spray would achieve the rhythmic motion of a conductor's baton, but with many changes of tempo. Different kinds of willow in the assembly responded in different ways. Pendent streamers of the weeping kind nodded and swept the ground, sometimes boldy in semi-circles and with a gentle caressing touch when a lull came.

As I watched this sylvan ballet and remembered how often I had experienced other visions of trees in motion; whispering poplars, pines bending to a gale, the roaring of a storm in the midst of a forest; I realised that however graceful trees may be as peaceful silhouettes in the landscape it is only when they spring to life and gesticulate in their several ways in response to the flow of air that they become most delightfully significant in our lives.

Light and Water

Surlingham, September 18th, 1974

A river, like the sea, gives life to every image reflected from its surface and it is this quicksilver element which provides so many moments of enchantment for voyagers, including those who thread the waterways of Broadland in the gentle days of autumn.

The play of light on rippled streams has inspired poets through the ages and here, in low flood plains where wind and tide run free, the lilt of conflict stirs the waters almost every minute of the day and night.

In any harbour, the mirrored hulls of ships, shimmering in a moving patchwork of gloom and richly coloured light, beguile the eye with beauty, surging and swelling, drifting with a wink of bubbles or a wash of weed. And from time to time the pulsing flicker of light on surrounding structures evokes fancies of Neptunes's realm.

This morning, at a quayside on the Yare, I watched the lazy dance of a network of light reflected from rather choppy wavelets on the white-painted prow of a Broads cruiser. The leaping loops of gold were essentially diamond-shaped, ever expanding and narrowing, sometimes with intricate and confusing overleaps like a flicker of skipping-ropes. At every point of intersection, this living lace fizzed with a thistle-head of spray which blew off in spindrift.

I was reminded of the basic elements of life seen under a microscope and could almost envisage the origin of life itself in some primeval interplay of light and water after this fashion. But in the sphere of human delight, I was transported to the moment of childhood's first meeting with the antic's of Tinker Bell, that will-o'-the-wisp fairy, or to more recent scenes figuring the filmy, fluttering abandon of go-go girls interpreting the joys of youth in music and dance.

John Sell Cotman

No crystal-gazer, J.S.C.
   Who looked on Norman Wiliam's land,
And yet a crystal quality
   Lay in the eyes that led his hand.
He saw a brooding storm in peace
   And pools of shade at day's high noon . . .
Rivers and leaves that could not cease
   To multi-mirror sun and moon.
Before his tranquil, level sight
   The majesty of edifice
Rose from the sward to cloud-capped height
   Against the blue of common bliss.
Arches and trees and weathered rocks,
   Ships on the sea, monastic towers,
Cottages, gateways, curious locks,
   Shared his brush with the humble flowers.
The canvas rich, the palette old,
   The shadow clear, the mirror dark,
The silver muted into gold—
   These bear the John Sell Cotman mark.
And through the maze of every view
   One sure line points the thing to see:
The rift, the beam, the bough, the dew,
   The distance of Eternity.

On seeing John Sell Cotman's paintings at
Norwich Castle Museum, 27th June, 1945.

In the Dark

February, 1975

Nightfall brings magic to country lanes. For the walker, listening to clump, clump of his own footsteps, so much is hidden in the folds of night, wrapped close in mystery when even whispers die and only owls are bold, like ghosts wakened from sepulchres to thrill again with eerie challenge.

Thick, dark-ivied trunks and snake-like branches are limned against the diffused pallor of clouds; scraggy umbrella trees seem carved in ebony with the orange glow of city lights like a false dawn behind them. Cottage gables become as weird and monumental as Stonehenge. Square window lights in the village are like lanterns viewed from a ship off the coast. Soft, cool air brings a reek of marsh mud like salt in the nostrils. Luminous dykes and puddles shine like the muted silver of armour.

Momentarily a little whisk of breeze sets bushes swaying with a lilt scarcely noticeable in the broad light of day. Down by the river a moorhen utters a shrill cry as though startled in a dream. There are wayside wraiths: winter's bleached grasses hovering and vanishing like the curtains of Aurora Borealis in a polar sky. To walk by night is to live again in that Eden where mice disport themselves in leafy ways and rabbits nibble in peace along the verges.

In earliest childhood, when I first heard of rooks cawing in the tree-tops after sunset, I asked my mother, 'What's in the dark?' and now, more than sixty years on in life, I still wonder.

Dancing Reeds

November, 1975

Wordsworth's daffodils, tossing their heads in sprightly dance, were small-time performers compared with Norfolk's graceful reeds, however delightful their setting in the green vistas of Lakeland.

Today, as I looked out to a fringe of marsh where tree-shadows formed a dark back-cloth and sunlight flooded an open area in front, some well-spaced reeds held the stage and displayed their perfect freedom of movement as the wind swirled about them. They looked for all the world like human dancers, swaying, writhing, bowing and thrusting. At times their gestures were those of a group of African braves leaning forward with levelled spears; then they were naiads rising from a pool with tresses flying in an abandon of feminine grace and pale arms pointing to the heavens. They sprang and stood still, like ballet-dancers on tiptoe, assuming classical postures only to pass into the wild whirling of a melee of dervishes as an eddy struck them.

There were moments when the stiff leaves streaked out horizontally and trembled or shuddered in a streaming breeze, and sometimes they fluttered like flags in the hand of a signaller, with a military rhythm.

The only music accompanying the reed dancers was their own whispering as they touched crisply in passing, and a faint murmuration of wind in the willows nearby; but the scene conjured up a sweetness of wandering harmonies in the mind: of flutes and panpipes and soft, crooning voices; of drums in the jungle and pibrochs in the hills, while I came to see in every ecstacy of the dances before me a parallel in human grace expressing the freedom of spirit that lies within us all.

The Smiling Sun

December, 1975

Even without the virgin wonder of snow, winter has its moments of rare beauty. Today has been filled with visions and vistas of the fairyland we knew as children.

The dawn glowed softly with a warmth of promise and lingered long by reflection on high clouds in the northern sky. Then the sun itself burned its way through the early haze, to throw the countryside into bright relief. Trees were revealed in all their intricate perfection as though part of a transformation scene on a floodlit stage, and farm buildings acquired the aura seen on rare old canvases.

As I drove into Norwich by way of Crown Point, the County Hall was shining full square like a castle of pale gold against the wooded hill of Bracondale while, far beyond, a pillar of fire glared, defiant, at the sun where the glass palace of an office tower broke the skyline. Later, as I walked about the city, I was conscious all the time of a peculiar quality in the atmosphere, like a brooding peace, for all the Christmas bustle of the streets.

From Barrack Street I found myself looking up to the grassy bastions of Mousehold with new delight, and from the old Cattle Market and the top of Rouen Road, country vistas across the valley appeared more serene and beautiful than ever before, though I have looked that way a thousand times.

I think the stillness had something to do with it, but principally it must have been the smiling of the sun into all the misty folds and creases of hill and dale, revealing pastel tints everywhere.

Tonight the magic held as the moon soared above a crisp and sparkling world, and near my home in the marshes only the quavering notes of an owl and the staccato 'prink' of a moorhen now and again gave voice to the ecstasy of winter's solitude.

Fairy Bonfires

October, 1976

Sedgy leaf-mats in hollows of the fen were crisp and powdered with frost in the stillness of dawn today, although the abundance of gossamer everywhere seemed to suggest that this chilling had occurred only at the brink of day. Presently the sun was flooding the scene as it soared above a bank of night clouds in the east.

Reeds drooping with beaded moisture glittered like a million mirrors; tall willow-herbs, brown and ragged, were laced with spider silk; here and there a streak of yellow, orange or fiery crimson enlivened the pattern of tousled marsh vegetation, and I saw the odd birch tree with leaves like flakes of gold painted on the canvas of the sky. Yet there was a bed of watercress still lush and vivid green nearby and graceful sedge tussocks by the water's edge as yet gave no hint of autumn's withering.

It soon became clear that the sun's warmth was making itself felt even in the depths of the hummocky undergrowth. As I surveyed the scene, it seemed almost as though scores of little geysers were producing bursts of steam at various points on the open fen, or that fairy bonfires were smouldering fitfully here and there. As puffs of vapour reached head height, they thinned to vanishing point, instead of blanketing the fen with mist.

My observations led me to believe that this localised production of steam was due to concentration of the sun's rays through some of the larger beads of water on vegetation, these having the same burning effect as a magnifying glass. The 'geyser' puffs were so intermittent and brief in duration individually that one had the impression of water being brought to the boil in minute quantities, as happens when drops of water are spilled on the hot top of a stove.

Sculpture in Ice

Surlingham, January 4th, 1977

I never cease to wonder at the endlessly varied forms assumed by the plates of ice which decorate the fringes of our marsh dykes whenever we have a spell of frosty weather.

The magic touch is applied by the rise and fall of the tides, whereby thin sheets of ice are left encrusting emergent reed stems, tree roots, floating mats of litter and driftwood when the water level drops. In the stillness of the night these ice plates develop crystal outgrowths which glitter like all the jewels of fairyland when morning light comes.

Some are like miniature tents of glass, either clear or opaque; many spread like silvery star fishes with webbed arms; there are scintillating fairies'-wand stars with long rays, glittering crescents, moth wing and bat wing shapes, long plumes lying side by side like the pinions of doves or seagulls, and delicate lobes and brackets with fine concentric lines or even bold zebra striping here and there.

In places where there are overhanging trees which contribute drips for part of the day, the encrustations beneath are different again; less frilly and feathery and more polished, rounded and beaded with globules of air. Depending on the height reached by the water on the following tide and on the strength of the frost, the ice sculpture changes from hour to hour and day to day. Sometimes the dykes become completely ice-locked, but even then the crystal growth continues with its fantastic embellishment.

In the Fens

Yesterday, as I drove home from March across the vast levels of Fenland, roads were icy wherever a few willows flung morning shadows astride them, and deep, straight drains were glazed and sparkling on either side; but the sun's warmth had dissolved the silver of hoar frost on meadows where fieldfares, redwings and peewits were dotted about, not appearing to do anything in particular.

Here and there the black soil was exposed in all its ancient richness, reminding one of that distant time when marsh and swamp vegetation crowded the Fenland basin in rich luxuriance, laying down its legacy of fertile earth much as forests of the Carboniferous age produced the treasure of coal.

As cloud shadows travelled across the landscape, they gave it life and something of its former grandeur, while the glint of gold on reeds huddling in the ditches and the bright aura of little groups of osiers and birches revived visions of long years ago when the Fen

Tigers were battling with ooze and flood to win a paradise for agriculture. So was the willowy beauty of untamed patches of wilderness retained as an unquenched spirit of the past.

This great tract of country may have an air of boundless desolation in the depths of winter or when autumn's mists lie upon it, but as I saw it on this cheerful morning, it had a friendly mien and a warmth generated by its maturity of pattern resulting from the hopeful toil of men over the centuries.

Breckland in Spring

April, 1977

Breckland in cloud and sunshine at the outset of spring has a beauty of its own, with every vista linking long times past with times present, while the mood of winter still lingers. Today, as I gazed at the mysterious meres sparklingly recreated by upsurging waters in the chalk after the barrenness of a drought, and saw the rich green spears of bulrushes coming into their own, with bobbing coot and duck swimming about them, I felt the pulse of the years and realised that even Time can miss a heart-beat and go smilingly forward again.

Last summer's parched sands were minutely starred with a thousand white blossoms along the old foot-ways: whitlow grass, mouse-ear chickweed and rue-leaved saxifrage, twinkling like diamonds on green velvet. Bracken, flattened by the storms of winter, lay like a rusty cloak on the heath, protecting and nursing the young fronds about to uncurl in delicate green. There were silver wands of birches, a splash of golden gorse here and there, and blackthorn scrub dazzling as snow.

Lone pines, grown to full stature, stood like ghosts of prehistory, with the dark ranks of their tribes gathered behind them and stretching away into the blue depths of the forests. Swallows sped by, fulfilling their age-old promise to return, like the curlews and the cuckoos voicing their triumph and their joy. As I watched a kestrel hovering above me, I felt rather like a wind-hoverer myself, suspended in eternity.

Magic from the Air

Surlingham, April 19th, 1977

Yesterday I flew in great comfort from Norwich Airport to Leeds and back, using what is nowadays very largely a commuter route for the men who staff oil rigs in the north. For the regulars, swift journeys in cloudland, with the jigsaw of fields, dark woods and silver threads of rivers glimpsed far below, appear to have little or no magic. The snug cabin becomes a flying cafe, with liquid refreshments and newspapers supplied to alleviate the boredom.

My excursions into the world of soaring birds are still occasional enough to provide a thrill as I peer through the nearest magic window. On the morning flight, I was entranced by the shadows flung across the landscape by trees and buildings; from a height of 8000 feet they looked disproportionately huge, with mysterious rings and U-shaped figures appearing in the midst of ploughland here and there. It was fascinating to look down on the chains of gravel pit lakes and the larger reservoirs and to compare old woodlands with the formal plantations of the Forestry Commission. The vast loneliness of the Fens became more real than any map could show.

On my return journey the lights were twinkling in towns and villages while at 11,000 feet we were still in the brightness of the evening sky. We crossed the Wash well out from the Lincolnshire coast, and presently I was able to look down on the whole complex of dunes and salt marshes stretching from Hunstanton to Weybourne, with the rustling of white waves like silver chasing at the sea's edge, and the slender ridges of Scolt Head and Blakeney Point gleaming with sunset gold-like coral reefs of a Pacific atoll enclosing the dark lagoons of salt flats at full flood tide. And only minutes later, our great purring shuttle from the skies was settling like a dove in a field all starred beyond with the fairy lamps of Norwich.

95

The Archaeologist

Give me the tilted house, the crooked street,
  The leaning corner where old cronies meet,
The eaves that droop o'er squalorous gulleys where
  The human jackal has his natural lair.

I love the town-cramped church, the oppressive pub,
  The beam-propped barracks of the city's hub
And cobbled lanes where shadows make a play
  Of all imagining that blinks by day.

I go where excavations yield the bones
  Of plague and where ecclesiastic stones
And warriors' relics shuffle off their age,
  Unfabling Truth to mollify the sage.

I roam the ancient hills and rise on wings
  To survey toppled henges, mystic rings
And title-deeds of Time-devoured toil
  Writ faint in fairy writing on the soil.

I'm slow to scoff at skittles and the like:
  They're nearly old, with halberd, spear and pike
And passing fast to that enchanted land
  Where Death and I exchange a bridging hand.

The art of gentle potters of the past,
  The stereotyped Acanthus leaf must last.
There's no one now like Omar with his Rose
  To muse on Time and still breathe in repose.

The best that's gone I'll cherish for my friends,
  Whichever way the warp of Progress bends.
I let no Epstein blind me to the truth:
  It takes a draft of Time to steady youth.

So let me play with immortality,
  E'en thought I try to seize it backwardly;
And if Today shall make a thing that's good,
  'Twill interest my future brotherhood.

(1955)

Breckland Oasis

Surlingham, May 17th, 1978

This afternoon I savoured the enchantment of one of the largest remaining ancient grass heaths in Suffolk breckland, almost as spacious as the green oasis devoted to the sport of kings at Newmarket, but largely covered by tall, rough grasses, patched here and there with dark hummocks of ling heather and withered bracken.

Scots pines from neighbouring plantations were invading this open space in some parts where the young trees had been successful in establishing themselves against a variety of odds, including rabbits and hares and critical differences in the nature of the ground itself. While much of the grass cover had uniform appearance, there were some much-nibbled stretches of dry, somewhat chalky land, where the vegetation was sparse and dwarfed.

This was a paradise of crisp, tangled ground-lichens which were spread in little hummocks of grey, brown and silver in a setting of mosses and fine, wiry grasses. Where loose sand was exposed there were swarms of minute plants such as rue-leaved saxifrage, white-flowered whitlow grass, dwarf forget-me-not, spring vetch and *Teesdalea,* somewhat resembling miniature candytuft.

In this area, where classic studies of Breckland grass heaths have been going on continuously for a great many years, I was shown some square enclosures fenced against rabbits over a long period. These contained a number of special plants native to this terrain and clearly able to come to perfection only because the rabbits had been excluded. In one such oasis I saw a quantity of moonwort, a dwarf but sturdy little fern closely related to the adder's tongue. Its leaf blades are divided into crescent shaped, yellowish-green lobes, and the spore-bearing spikes are much branched.

Moonwort is rare in East Anglia nowadays, although it would doubtless flourish more widely were it not for the pressure of rabbit grazing. I had last seen it in a very different setting, perched on the black basalt crest of a Scottish mountain.

Sand-sculpture

Surlingham, July 15th, 1978

The rippling of sands on our beaches can be a great source of delight when tides have receded. They are to be seen in wonderful diversity along those parts of the coast where adjacent saltmarshes and underlying beds of clay ensure that water continues to seep and flow down to the sea, often via 'lows' between a succession of sand banks.

The pattern of vein-like channels cut through sloping beaches is similar, in miniature, to that which is typical of deltas in general, but as the streaming lessens towards extreme low tide, great numbers of the temporary watercourses cease their flow altogether and the 'lows' also become mere wet, sandy hollows. It is in the beds of these streamways that one sees the most spectacular undulations of sand-sculpture, involving every conceivable variation in crest and hollow, scalloped by the interacting forces of ebbing waters and irregular flurries of sea breezes.

One day last week, at Brancaster, I kept watch on the flow of runnels as they flowed down beach slopes and was able to see how their sculpting was achieved. Pebbles of various sizes, some of them very small, were scattered over the area and often impeded the flow, sometimes causing diversions, but more usually arresting the progress of the little streams quite briefly. Whenever such an obstruction was encountered, the water level built up to a peak and then curled back in a surging crest. This had the effect of scooping out the bed of the channel just behind the obstruction, loosening its hold, whereupon small stones were then swept forward, coming to rest shortly afterwards in the shallows.

This process was repeated many times, resulting in the carving of channels in a series of ups and downs. Sometimes a puff of wind caused a momentary change of course and this again left its mark in rippled sand. When the tide comes in, all patterns are defaced; but the process starts again with every ebb and each time there is a new display of intricate rippling, whose permutations are infinite.

Morning Fragrance

Surlingham, July 26th, 1978

One of the rewards of early rising in the country is the lingering fragrance that comes from grass, trees and flowers still wet with the night's dew. At this time of the year there is probably more sweetness in the morning air than at any other season, since there is a profusion of wild flowers and lush foliage almost everywhere. Some scents are deliciously pervasive: honeysuckle and sweet briar, for instance, while a stroll near marshland brings immediate acquaintance with the vanilla perfume of massed meadow-sweet blossoms.

A field of flowering horse beans also produces a powerful vanilla scent. In wet places there is the peppermint distillation of water mint. The pale, crowded flowers of elder and wild privet yield a rather heavy odour which is not to everyone's liking. The bog myrtle which abounds in many of the fens in Broadland has a very special resinous fragrance, often commented on by those who roam our waterways in summer. In wooded areas the scent of pines is often dominant and stimulating, with the call of the wild in it. The grasses which give a distinctive fragrance to new-mown hay can also be smelt as warm vapours rise from the meadows on a sunny morning.

To enjoy some of the more delicate scents of individual flowers one has to sniff them more closely. Some of the thistles, for instance, smell of cinnamon, and as the pink and white trumpets of corn bindweed unfold they have an almond scent, like that of certain spotted orchids in the meadows. Many flowers appearing at different seasons have similar odours. Meadow rue smells of primroses, and the white jasmine of the garden mimics lilies of the valley. Even the earth itself gives off musky vapours, derived, strangely enough, from soil bacteria.

Lonely Trail

Surlingham, October 16th, 1978

I travelled by rail to Cambridge today, in one of those coaches which permits a wide view of the countryside. I always find this journey a delight, in that it provides glimpses of much wilder and far flung landscapes in Breckland and the Fens that can be seen from the tarmac trail, with its hedges, tree belts and roadside clusters of homesteads.

The trains pursue a lonely path for many miles on end between stops which themselves are often near tiny oases in the wilderness. At this time of year the rusting bracken of the heaths glows richly against the darkness of forest pines. From time to time there are crossings of little rivers, with green meadows and pools thronged with snowy gulls. At Brandon there are the vast long piles where the forest gold is heaped from its perpetual harvest.

Then, after making passing acquaintance with the Little Ouse and its marshes, rounding off the meeting line of breck and fen, the trail leads through a vast and fantastic kingdom of poplars which stand in neat ranks stretching away into the far distance. Although these trees are present in tens of thousands, forming huge blocks, one can still see the bright horizon through them and many of the features of the countryside, even with half a mile of tree screen in the way. This is because the trunks are straight and well spaced and the leafy crowns far enough above the ground for the light to pass though their dappled aisles; and the floor of the poplar forest is green, for the same reason, with its carpet of vegetation.

I have heard that, on occasion, golden orioles have found a haven of delight in this airy land of the poplars. Beyond, there are black fens and dykes, seemingly a great sea of land, on whose desolate acres pied lapwings catch the light like foam-flecked wavelets here and there, while only larks and hovering kestrels rise high enough to survey with any acuteness the patterns of the fenman's limitless kingdom.

Woodland Magic

Surlingham, February 14th, 1979

On such a day as this one appreciates the shelter of trees and hedges. Late this afternoon I took a walk in comparative comfort while a blizzard was raging, simply by hugging the lee side of a wood.

I soon discovered that birds were like-minded since almost the first thing to attract my attention was a flock of bluetits sheltering in a clump of rhododendrons at the very edge of the wood. Looking to the west across a wide and rising sweep of ploughland I saw clouds of snow smoking and swirling like spindrift whipped from wave crests in a storm at sea, veiling the horizon in a shimmering screen so that the snowscape seemed to be merged with the sky.

Presently, on entering the wood, I found that a magical calm prevailed. The undergrowth of arched brambles and tumbled bracken was humped with snow, and paths were virgin white without even the imprint of any bird or small animal's feet. The tiers of hazel boughs with their slender twigs were all delicately ridged with snow, making a silver filigree which appeared luminous against a background of dark evergreens here and there.

Trunks of trees were whitened on one side. Smooth beeches achieved the grace of marble statuary, while the rough bark of oaks was clothed in crocodile scales of snow. Only the tree tops were astir in the blizzard wind. They were gathering no snow, but merely arresting its progress so that flakes were falling quite gently into the haven of calm below.

Snow World

Surlingham, February 15th, 1979

This morning I trudged through the snow drifts in a blizzard, sheltered only here and there by tall hedges, which are all too scarce nowadays. Not since 1947 have there been such vast snowfields spread across our countryside. Along the byways graduated wedges of snow extend downwind of every obstruction.

Some fields are clothed with a level white blanket while on others there are frozen billows or else swarms of hummocky snow puffs reminding one of miniature igloos. The wind swirling round corners creates bluffs and sheer cliffs, contrasting with the gentle curves of mounds and hollows elsewhere. As I passed along the village street, glimpsing white-capped homes and snow-blotched windowpanes, it seemed that life had come to a standstill. I almost expected to hear the tinkling of sleigh-bells.

Turning towards the river I waded down a causeway to Coldham Hall, isolated by floods. Moorhens were swimming over the road in front of me and water rails squealed from cover in the adjacent marshes. For some distance a robin followed me, hopeful that I would disturb something small and edible that might catch his eye. On one side lay a swamp filled with water-soaked snow soiled with the stain of mud so that it looked like crystallised honey. On the opposite side the fen vegetation, drooping at all angles under its silver capping, obscured the rising floodwaters.

I noticed a thicket of sallow bushes whose wind whipped upper twigs were blown against the sky while lower down in shelter, they formed a zone of white with a dark pool below. The overall effect reminded me of a cream-filled chocolate sandwich. Having reached the riverside inn and enjoyed a brief respite by its fireside, I retraced my steps precariously along the causeway just in time to escape a soaking. A I turned to go, waves were breaking over the quay and I was warned that the tide would be rising for a further three hours.

Modesty

Surlingham, May 4

*I once had the temerity to suggest that
perhaps mosquitoes rather than modesty
persuaded Adam and Eve to clothe
themselves. Modesty, nevertheless, in its
broader sense, is an essential sweetener of
human attitudes as they affect the future of
the world about us. Today I offer two short
poems reflecting on this theme.*

ICONOCLASM

In professions Zoologic,
  Geologic, Mycologic
And even Ichthyologic,
  The arrogant are few.
All Science, of whatever -ic
  Is still so Embryologic,
It is but Anthropologic,
  To take a humble pew.
In classy circles Politic
  (Democratic, Bureaucratic,
Pluto- and Aristocratic)
  They take another view.
The Chosen swank of any -ic
  And go to lengths quite Lunatic
To reach a state Autocratic,
  While all else goes askew.

ANCESTORS

My fathers had a hand in everything;
  For good, for shame, I owe them all a bit:
The ace, the knave, the joker and the king;
  The dullard, dastard and the merry wit.
Some wed their cousins rather close
  And lagged where vineyards tempted them to peace;
Their tribes grew gentle nations in repose
  Such as the roving hordes were wont to fleece.
Those ancestors were such a motley crew,
  Working for freedom and for bondage both
And bubbling from their sweet and bitter brew,
  I come to choose a way and plight a troth.

Cosy Harbour

Reydon, Suffolk, May 21st, 1979

Although Southwold is no longer a busy port, the spirit of its halcyon days lives on where seafaring craft capable of negotiating its constricted harbour are hauled up in great array along the Black Shore.

Their deep keels and the smooth sharpness of their prows speak of adventure, and their bright paintwork contrasts with the tarry blackness of piles and staging where bladderwrack bobs on the tide and the strand is littered with rusting anchors, old ropes and spars, mud and cockleshells.

When we strolled that way in the evening the sea was very restful. The day had been warm and the tang of salt in the air was spiced with the fragrance of sea wormwood fringing the river, and feathery clumps of fennel and hay-scented melilot growing along the sea bank. A common tern alighted on a post, screaming what proved to be an invitation to her mate to bring a love offering in the shape of a fish, which was proffered and accepted a moment later.

Upstream by the Blyth estuary, its saltings carpeted with sea lavender, sea aster, arrow-grass now spiky with tall green flower heads and swarms of tiny crimson and scarlet seedlings of the samphire which will clothe wet mud in greenery when summer comes. A vast and lonely marshscape in the background, the gold of gorse on Reydon Common on the northern flank and the patchwork of undulating heath and woodland to the south, all serve to emphasise the human cosiness of the little harbour, and its enchantment for those who contrive adventures on the sea.

Magical Dawn

Surlingham, June 6th, 1979

This morning I chanced to rise rather earlier than usual, a little over half-an-hour before dawn, and in the grey of fast fading night, ventured forth into the magical atmosphere of calm and expectancy which is a prelude to all other delights of a summer's day.

There was dew on the grass and a rich fragrance of flowers in the garden. Blackbirds were in full song in the trees round about, as were cuckoos further afield, while the cooing of doves had already commenced, wrens uttered staccato trills on awakening and the crowing of a cock pheasant burst explosively from a thicket.

Dozens of pipistrelle bats were just then returning to their roost under the pantiles of an outhouse which they use for a nursery every summer. For awhile they circled dizzily at speed as each one awaited its chance to alight and disappear through the one narrow entrance. Bumble bees were already collecting nectar and I found that one loud hum was coming from a queen wasp visiting cotoneaster blossoms at 4 a.m. Small white moths were still dancing round the sweetly scented flowers of a burnet rose and others were visiting the lacy heads of cow parsley where they had shared sweets with mosquitoes in the night.

Presently, as the silvering of marsh vapours cleared with the stirring of a cool little breeze, a golden light suffused the heavens and day had come, by gentle stealth, with the sun beaming upon a green and happy world.

Nightfall, too

Surlingham, June 7th, 1979

Having experienced the enchantments of dawn (yesterday), I made a point of savouring the delights of nightfall at the end of a perfect June day. As the sun dipped, casting long shadows, the first sweat of dew was gathering on the grass as it chilled.

An hour before sundown daisies and buttercups, bird's-eyes and stars of Bethlehem were closing and the dampness on dandelion clocks prevented any further bid for freedom by the parachute seeds. But the blossoming hawthorns continued to scent the air and delicate fragrances drifted from ragged robin and the milk-white flowers of guelder rose on the fen, where yellow flags could be seen gleaming here and there among the reeds, now a vivid green and standing breast high. Blackbirds fluted again from their favourite perches and turtle doves purred away to the accompaniment of the bellowing of cattle in a nearby pasture and the final shouts of pheasants going to roost. For a while, swifts sped across the darkening heavens as swallows made their last sallies before retiring to their nests. Presently I heard the grunting of a woodcock as it sped round in circles in roding flight.

As I waited for the first bats to emerge, I could see spiders weaving new cartwheel webs, silhouetted among the branches. The bats loitered for almost twenty minutes after sunset before venturing forth and dashing for the woods; I wondered at first if perhaps the evening air was too cool to tempt them out, although gnats and moths were darting about everywhere. A pale moon riding in the southern sky was obscured at times by small ragged clouds which seemed to portend the approach of rain; but the threat failed to materialise and the night proved sweet and peaceful, like the day.

Spirit of Youth

September, 1979

As I am writing, I often steal a glance through my study window to contemplate the form of a weeping willow: a tree of many graces. On a calm evening, its long, pendulous wands dip to the grass as sheerly as a plumb-line from high-arched boughs, amber-bright in winter and trimmed with slender leaves from April to October. Although so gentle in repose, this supple tree is set in motion by the slightest tremor of wind.

From gentle, tip-toe idling, in pensive mood, with a swaying of its shoulders, and leaves lightly fluttering against the blue of the sky above, it may be stirred to engage in a fairy dance as silken tresses stream out a little, like delicate cascades of spray from a waterfall. Under the influence of somewhat bolder breezes the leafy wands flow horizontally to leeward, while those taking the greater strain swing to and fro, bowing and lifting or sweeping in gracious curves, flouncing, flopping and shivering on the rebound. In a gusty wind, the fluid ripples give place to gallops, with a frisky lifting of green skirts and more than a touch of abandonment as tresses are tossed and sinuous boughs swing one way and another.

But it takes a gale to bring the most exciting response in this supple dancer, as her crown flashes silver against lowering storm clouds. Pitching and tossing, the boughs recoil and spring, gyrating in torment, while the wands simulate the angry lashings of a tiger's tail where the full fury of the wind smites them and even beneath, they become engaged in dervish dances, with leaves whirling madly and from time to time snaking like the tails of kites in silhouette.

Whether in repose or pawing the sky in passion, a solitary weeping willow conjures up the spirit of youth in all its moods and remains forever young in image, a symbol of the resilience of life, thrilling with the turmoil of battle against the elements, responding with a frolic under lighter strain and relaxing to assume a stance of pensive innocence in quiet moments.

Pool of Paradise

Surlingham, October 22nd, 1979

One day last week I was introduced to an enchanting lake, fed by springs and the little River Mun at Templewood, set among the wooded hills of Northrepps. Except for the ripples made by fish in the waters and the movement of a red or golden leaf here and there where a slight breeze smote the surface, peace reigned in a dream world where the amphitheatre of trees and palisades of still green reeds were reflected in the mirror of the pool.

Those who cherish this hidden sanctuary know times when the jewelled kingfisher haunts the shores, uttering its sharp whistle from regular stances as it makes its rounds. In winter, teal and other wildfowl drop out of the sky to enjoy a respite from the alarums of flight-pools and coastal creeks where the guns bark. In hard weather, woodcock shelter under the trees and venture forth to probe the valley grasslands for earthworms with their sensitive beaks. Even fairly recently, I was told, otters have been moving in the vicinity and may at any time return to a perfect habitat, unsullied and undisturbed, with fish in abundance to satisfy their appetites.

Landscaped with skill and devotion by the late Viscount Templewood, who lived long enough to see the woods he planted taking shape and to enjoy the central vista of his creation, this retreat among the glacial undulations of north-east Norfolk is cared for still by those whose lives it warms across the years, and though contrived, it is a paradise for wildlife as well as satisfying the vision of man in creative and artistic ways.

Curtains of Snow

December 7th, 1980

We might have known that snow flurries would be sweeping upon us out of the North, when, a few nights ago, wild swans woke us with their trumpeting overhead. Icy winds were quick to follow, with gales of sleet, and last night, hail rattled down to cloak the countryside in a crunchy, crystallised covering. This morning all was a-glitter as the sun shone from a sky of wintry blue, but towering cumulus clouds still moved across the scene, with smoky skirts and dark smurs of recurrent squalls reaching down like curtains here and there.

On a short walk down to the Fen, I discovered contrasting beauty in mosaics of russet, yellow and purple foliage on wild privet and bramble, where interlaced bines and twigs gleamed like bright threads in the thickets.

Dyke-sides were palisaded with bleached reeds boldly plumed and still hung with down-sloping leaves, some sweating with newly-melted ice and others withered to dryness, stiff and shrunken in the form of slender spears. Out of the direct impact of sunbeams, all undergrowth lay congealed in every kind of crystal tracery, except where a high tide brimming over banks seeped snakily into hollows and sunken paths, softening black ooze and entrapping bubbles of marsh gas in a thin scum.

As I splashed and crunched my way along a dyke-side, the soggy track was fringed and criss-crossed with jutting fragments of dead plants, including many a gracefully turned

strand of grass and sedge, loaded above with diamond dust and dripping with silver droplets. Even in sheltered places, there was the sharp tingle of cold in the air; but this seemed in no way to retard the movements of small birds such as reed buntings, wrens and blue tits foraging in reed and bush, while blackbirds and fieldfares were much in evidence, hastening to strip every gleaming berry glimpsed in the cosiness of thickets. I saw no flight of ducks silhouetted overhead, but from time to time scattered flocks of wood pigeons appeared, making for the woods where they could be sure of feasting on the still lavish spread of fallen acorns, albeit partly overspread by a white carpet under the leaf-bare trees.

Glossary

Noah's Ark: Cirrus clouds running parallel like the planks of a ships hull.
Flags: Yellow irises.
Carnser: Causeway.
Pulk-holes: Small deep pools hidden in swamps.
Dike: in this case, a ditch filled with water.
Gnat-hills: Sedge tussocks, above the crowns of which, smoke-like columns of gnats are wont to dance on summer evenings.
Golleston: Gorleston, at the mouth of the river Yare, debouching on the North Sea.

Sonnet to a young partner at a winter festivity.

Invitation to the Marsh

He
That Noah's ark ha' passed away:
   Tha's time to be a-goin.
We'll have a good old jam today
   An' p'raps a mite o' rowin'.

Come on, m' dear; the sun 'on't wait.
   I'll show ye where the flags grow.
If we go quick, we sha'n't be late
   (Unless we find the tide low!)

Ye'll hev to mind yar step a bit
   When we git off the carnser:
Them pulk-holes ent the place to set
   Except for a' ol harnser—

An' even he stand wary-like
   An' keep his mind on lookin',
Or else he might flop in a dike
   An' git a proper sookin'!

I mind the time I lost m' way
   In one of them ole night fogs
An' had to wait till light o' day
   A-listenin' to the ole frogs!

That wouldn't've done to move a inch
   Wi' gnat-hills all around me.
I might ha' tried it at a pinch,
   But no-one wouldn't've found me.

Now, if I've frightened ye, m' dear
   I'll take ye on the river.
If we shoot out by Go'leston' pier
   Ye'll hev to mind y'r liver!

She
Oh Alfred y're a one, you are!
   I ain't a water-spaniel.
I'm goin' in a mootty-car
   Along o' y'r brother Dan'l!

The Garden City

Surlingham, March 25th, 1981

Yesterday morning an hour's enforced idleness in Norwich allowed me to enjoy an early burst of sunshine to the full as I strolled without any set mission in mind, pausing to take a second look at anything which happened to catch my interest.

Not having acquired the habit of window-shopping, I found myself taking note of the colours and shapes of buildings in the mass and the textures of flint, brick and tiles, while stains of moss and algae and weeds of the crannies and neglected corners received a probing glance.

Suddenly, at a crossing, I was confronted by a bed of multi-coloured polyanthus. In a flash I was taken back to my first encounter with these exotic, bright-eyed primroses as a child.

Gold, scarlet, crimson and purple, rich as velvet, they seemed at that moment more glorious than all other flowers I had encountered in the wild or in gardens.

The memory of that happy surprise goes back close on 70 years. Since then, I have seen many new and giant varieties of polyanthus developed, including blue ones, and have come to miss the gold-laced forms which had a royal splendour lacking in many of their successors; but they all continue to give me special delight.

Having taken my fill of beauty at the traffic island, I went on to feast my eyes on the flowers displayed in Norwich Market.

There, fresh as the morning dew and aglow in the spring sunshine, were galaxies of daffodils and blushing tulips, bunched alongside violets, carnations, crimson rosebuds, freesias and rainbow-bright anemones, their colours everywhere enhanced by the delicate greenery of ferns.

There were stalls loaded with pot plants, many of them culled from far-off jungles and other paradises of tropical lands.

Here again, I experienced recapture of early thrills on seeing displays of cinerarias, with their startlingly pure, rich colours and white, daisy centres.

It is difficult to convey in words this joy that comes from recognising the favourites of childhood; perhaps it can be likened to hearing again some old sweet song.

Leafy Blizzard

Surlingham, November 24th, 1981

A darkening sky presaged the onslaught of fierce squalls and downpours yesterday afternoon. As the wind gained strength the woods adjoining my house moaned and roared like the rigging of a thousand ships caught in a storm at sea.

In their pitching and tossing, trees everywhere were stripped of leaves, while those already littering the ground were whisked high into the air so that at times they filled the heavens, darting and diving like flocks of swallows in ecstasy, while in the lulls they drifted down like huge snowflakes. Never before had I seen so many leaves in the air at once.

Those that ultimately found refuge in sheltered hollows soon lay knee-deep, but even when rain-soaked, those alighting in exposed places found no peace: they created ever-changing mosaics of brown, gold and green, seeming to pulse and stir like restless butterflies, enacting such a scene as is created every autumn by the migratory hordes of Monarchs clustering about the trees of Florida preparatory to hibernation.

I saw trunks of lone trees the surface of whose bark threw off a spindrift of hissing raindrops on either side, while flying leaves, arrested for a moment in collision so as to appear held by force against the barriers, soon scudded to rejoin their companions. After the storm was over I inspected two marsh dykes at the rear of my garden and found them piled high with leaves, many of which still rode above the surface, not having had time to settle down into the already brimfull watercourse.

On a morning walk through the woods I had already encountered thick beds of leaves hiding the mosses and festooning the boughed fronds of bracken and although the later turbulence will have caused some violent stirrings there, the end result must be cumulative in the more sheltered fastnesses away from the exposed western fringe.

Sea of Silver

Surlingham, December 27th, 1981

Our white Christmas came to dazzling perfection yesterday morning when, as the misty cloak of night was lifted, we discerned silver rime transfiguring every leaf and twig from tree top to sward.

The Fen, still billowy with snow, had the appearance of an angry, foaming sea with wave-crests of wind-tousled vegetation seeming to curl in leaping plumes of spray. The snow itself had acquired a fresh covering of ice spicules which had grown to glittering beauty in the night, standing out from the virgin surface like starry lobes of moss, glinting like a great shower of diamonds. Snow-clotted umbels of angelica standing stiffly here and there looked as though they were in flower again, but the prone stalks of giant marsh sowthistles accompanying some of them belied this, lying there like warriors slain and abandoned in winter's battles.

Walking through the woods, while the air was still piercingly cold, I paused to examine the embroidery of the frost neatly edging the evergreen leaves of holly and rhododendrons and to marvel at the glittering traceries on birch and oak. Hazel catkins, already well formed, looked as though they had been dipped in icing sugar. Footprints of birds, rabbits and grey squirrels were clearly defined, their edges now rigid in the grip of the frost, like the snow carpet itself.

Presently the sun came out, and within an hour the rime on twigs had vanished, congealing into beads of water which, falling like heavy raindrops, produced an incessant musical patter as they hit the frosted snow beneath. Where sunshine flooded the south facing slopes of the snow mounds some thawing was achieved, and where trees overhung these illuminated patches the surface soon became pitted by the descending drips. As time went on the craters widened until the snow appeared curiously honeycombed. In this chill December every day has brought some fresh beauty to the wintry scene, compensating us for miseries endured.

Home From Home

Surlingham, February 22nd, 1982

I experience a glow of pleasure whenever, at this time of the year, I renew acquaintance with the many-flowered little *Narcissus tazetta,* ssp. *aureus* which goes by the name 'Soleil d'Or.'

Its stiffly prim gold perianths, cupped with orange coronets in their centres, give forth a fragrance as sweet as any Roman hyacinth. They come to us, bunched for the market, from the Scillies, the Channel Islands and other places warmed early by the sunshine that hastens the coming of spring in the south, while some are nurtured under glass. To see them growing truly wild, one has to visit the meadows of certain parts of France and Italy and they can be encountered widely naturalised in other lands bordering the Mediterranean, along with others of their tribe, often in great profusion.

Their special attraction for me stems from my first discovery of a cluster of them in my Guernsey garden when I was five years old. They were a wonder of wonders and that first savouring of their delights is re-captured anew whenever I meet with them, by special intent, year after year. Many of us have our favourite flowers, which may be wild or cultivated kinds, and I believe that this choice is often dictated by a vivid experience of the pleasure they have given when first discovered early in life.

The floral riches of our gardens have been gathered from all the world and similarly, our human population of England has cosmopolitan origins nowadays. So, when strangers from afar find sanctuary in this green island, whether their childhood was spent in far Cathay, the African veldt, Tierra del Fuego, the summery West Indies or frozen Alaska, they will be sure to meet again, in an English garden, some jewel from their native wilderness which reminds them of home.

Seaside Gravel Pits

June 3rd, 1965

Suffolk: Gravel pits can be rather unsightly, but when they become derelict, nature often clothes their crags with blossoming scrub, their spoil heaps come to look like natural, grassy knolls studded with a wealth of wild flowers in season, while the flooded hollows are soon teeming with aquatic life. I have just visited a group of such pits on the Suffolk coast at Benacre. Since they were abandoned just after the last war the sea has broken into some of them from time to time and as a result of this there is a fascinating assortment of marine, brackish and freshwater life in the various pools, while the surrounding vegetation is similarly mixed. In one reed-fringed pit, for instance, I found thousands of young edible mussels attached to the tangled filaments of a green algae and the coiled, black, sandy castings of lugworms were visible at the bottom. An adjoining pit had been colonised by pond-weeds and sticklebacks. Although the site was many miles distant from the nearest natural salt marshes, I found 'lows' carpeted with sea milkwort and widely colonised by sea aster. High bluffs of shingle on the landward side were yellow with gorse at its best and some of the slopes were almost as brilliant with the yellow blossoms of silverweed, creeping right down to the water's edge. Considerable reed beds had developed in the shallower parts of the flooded pits and these had their reed warblers and reed buntings in residence.

The uneven ground round about was patched with tiny forget-me-nots, a scarlet-leaved mossy stonecrop, a small pale chickweed, grey hair-grass and a miniature spring vetch with amethyst flowers, with vari-coloured lichens on the sands between clumps of bird's-foot trefoil and blue dog violets. These gravel pits had become a paradise.

Will-o'-the-wisp Time

July 1st, 1965

Norfolk: At sundown on soft June evenings the marshes round the broads often become clothed with a white mist. This is sometimes curiously patchy and oddly stratified so as to produce miragelike effects by which dark trees and bushes seem to be standing in huge silver lakes, while distant reeds appear magnified and yet half dissolved in cloudland. I walked home along a marsh track recently at this will-o'-the-wisp time of the night, feeling alternate draughts of hot and cold air on my face and inhaling an assortment of pungent fragrances

which were wafted from beds of water mint, nettles and marsh hay. A grasshopper warbler purred away like a spinning-wheel from the heart of a lonely sallow bush. Female glow-worms twirled their tail-lights in dark recesses beneath grass tufts. Yellow flag irises looked faintly luminous where they stood in hundreds among the sedges and tall, primrose-tasselled, rose-scented meadow rues.

Above one distant bush a dark column of gnats rose like smoke from a funeral pyre, sometimes eddying and swirling like a column of starlings about to settle in a reed bed for the night. I came upon a ditch-side burdock so huge and statuesque against its background of snow-white mist that for a moment I felt like Gulliver travelling in Brobdingnag. My foot slipped on a large black slug and just as I was recovering equilibrium a splendid ghost swift moth dashed out of the shadows and brushed my face. Small, pale moths zig-zagged erratically over the marsh vegetation which was by now silvered with dew. As I approached the end of the track, where the day's fallen petals of wild rose littered the ground, I felt a cool breeze stirring and, looking back, I discovered that the mist had vanished already from all but a few tree-sheltered hollows of the marshland.

Glow-worm Saga

June 16th, 1966

Norfolk: Glow-worms used to twinkle by the thousand on damp rushy commons and mowing-marshes in East Anglia forty years ago. As a boy I remember some magical rambles on soft June nights when sweet briar was fragrant along the lanes and natterjack toads were scuttling about like mice on tracks leading to the glow-worms' haunts. I have stood in the midst of a rush-meadow and seen the pale faces of galaxies of marsh orchids reflecting the light from scores of little phosphorescent lamps glowing and twirling from dew-laden grass stems all round me. Here and there twin flashes like pin-points of flame would flicker in the air where winged male beetles assembled like fireflies attracted by the beckoning females. Brilliant scenes like this are now a thing of the past. Much of the terrain which glow-worms found attractive is no longer suited to their needs. Fenny meadows are not mown in summer now to provide litter for horses, so they have become overgrown with tall meadowsweet and reeds and bushes; or else they have been drained and cultivated.

After the Ball

Sonnet to a young partner at a winter festivity

Like Harlequin, I say, dear Columbine:
You lit a candle for me in a secret shrine!
   A candle with a strangely warming light
   Which dances and comes near me in the night.

The dark is dimpled; one carnation glows
And, soft, I touch the satin of a rose.
   I was a prince and Cinderella gone;
   But, Tinker Bell, you'll come again anon?

The poetry of hearts has slipped its cage:
That which was old in childhood knows not Age.
   Stars in their courses hold; the Heavens are mute;
   A nightingale evokes a magic flute.

And in this mystery I feel the hand
That stole away with me to Fairyland
   Where, in the dance, bewitched by every grace
   I found a keepsake in your smiling face.

This is not the whole story, however. I believe that the glow-worm population suffers very seriously from the circumstances which now interfere with the process of courtship. The males are commonly seduced by lights in houses and the dazzling headlamps in cars. As a result of this, many females are condemned to spinsterhood. There are still a few glow-worms on fens near my own in Broadland; but they are relatively scarce except in my garden nowadays. I believe this is because the females stand their best chance of securing mates where the males are attracted by the house light at night and find their true loves at hand when we have retired to bed.

On Dunwich Heath

November 16th, 1967

Suffolk: As we came over the crest of the heath overlooking Dunwich Bay this morning, the cold of winter was in the air, bleaching and curling the rust-red bracken and withering tattered leaves on the wind-stagged oaks; but presently we found the golden warmth of autumn lingering in a marshy valley and looked at the sea through a haze engendered by sunshine on a wilderness of reeds. A harrier floated and flapped in far silhouette where larks crouched low on the heath and we heard the 'chinking' notes of bearded tits in the shelter of the reed beds. Following a sandy track below a pine and chestnut wood, we came upon a paradise of rabbits, where close nibbling had preserved space for a rich array of silver-green and scarlet-clubbed lichens and a million starry moss-cushions. Here we disturbed a few late grasshoppers still clinging hopefully to life, but they were too lethargic to hop aside from our path. Here and there a bramble had burst into blossom afresh and close beside one flowering spray we found a full-grown, softly furry caterpillar of the Oak Eggar moth curled in splendour. As we climbed again to a little knoll capped with elm-scrub, we noticed bright green leaves of *Montia perfoliata* carpeting the ground in a seedling swarm; growing on through the dull days of the next few months, they will brighten the scene with snowy flowers at winter's end. Brushing our way through stiff, dark, tufts of broom and crimson-leaved brambles, we descended to a salt creek lined with silver-fluffing sea asters and followed a thin line of dunes to a little harbour-waste such as Peggotty knew along this East coast in the unsophisticated long-ago.

A Winter Ramble

14th December, 1967

Norfolk: The ploughland was pink and snow-dappled; a pheasant, warming to the sunrise, stood in the hedge-bottom, burnished, iridescent, as it stretched one wing. I was dazzled by touches of rime and gossamer as I watched a magpie prancing in a golden mist. To the east lay a meadow, green but for edging cloud-shapes and fingers of snow still in shadow. Skirting a lowland ditch brimming with blue water I put up a snipe from a patch of rushes and as it shrieked in curving flight I also heard the 'smee-oo' whistling of a bunch of wigeon hurrying from a nearby pool. I plunged into the reed-marshes nearer the river and found them brightly and rather delicately plated with ice spread in well-spaced layers where successive tidal floods had left their frozen tops stretched between supporting reed-stalks.

I followed a path through the reeds. Suddenly a dark cloud filled the whole valley with gloom and in the next five minutes the crystal of ice sheets lay smothered under a thick covering of hailstones. Now the marsh about me seemed to be draped in ermine as it shone again under a blue sky. I waded through swirling water where otters had worn a track letting off a flood between two ancient alders; and where the waters ran, they lapped against vertical plates of ice, fretting and honeycombing the edges and revealing strange crystal patterns of crosses and chrysanthemum leaves. Now again the ice-flaps hinged on reeds and twigs, creaked like the timbers of a yacht under strain. As another squall approached I heard the singing wing-beats of a herd of swans and looked up to take my fill of winter's magic as the great birds sped on their majestic way, like angels of light fleeing from the gathering gloom.

Airship Adventure

June 11th, 1968

Norfolk: When the Goodyear airship 'Europa' visited Norwich recently, I was privileged to take a flight in her over the broads, fens and woods near my home in the Yare Valley. Travelling at a gentle pace, with the golden glow of evening enhancing every detail of land and water beneath, we seemed to float and hover like a cloud in an otherwise cloudless sky, pausing or nosing down at will to inspect anything of peculiar interest. Vegetation patterns in the wetland areas were well defined, with bright green water grass bordering pools and winding channels, tracts of pale gold, winter-bleached reed and dark thickets of alder and sallow encroaching on the more open ground. There were well marked lines of old alders established on ridges once used by the peat-diggers who excavated the broads over 500 yers ago. Wild ducks on the waterways appeared as mere specks, chiefly noticeable from the occasional glitter of ripples as they moved, while swans and gulls, being white, were conspicuous, though dwarfed to the size of butterflies. We looked down on the hulks of a cluster of sunken wherries, once a familiar sight as they sailed the local rivers. Although aerial mapping and photography provide a valuable coverage for landscape features, they can never compare with what can be seen from an airship ambling at leisure. I have flown over the broads more than once in a light aircraft and on one occasion espied from a height of a thousand feet a kingfisher travelling steadily along a straight track, like a brillaint blue bead. From 'Europa' I scanned the jewelled mosaic below in vain for a repetition of this delight. Kingfishers, alas, are far from common along our waterways at this time.

Easter Adventure

April 2nd, 1970

Norfolk: It might be winter still on the Broads, with vistas of pale reeds and leafless willows and not a glimpse yet of king-cups or yellow catkins. At Easter we paid an evening visit to friends dwelling in solitude on an island looking out upon what could well have been taken for one of the mysterious swamp lakes of the Everglades on this occasion. Although this broad is normally thronged with yachts by day people steal away from it before nightfall and the peace of the wilderness settles upon it. To reach the island we threaded our way in a small boat through a swamp of dark and stately alders, thence emerging from a bay to cross still waters with a path of sunset gold limning black coot and lone cygnet. Across the middle of the lake black-headed gulls were settling to roost in a long white line, bright as the crest of a wave and no doubt likely to be relatively inconspicuous when darkness settled. Presently, having negotiated the hazards of a slimy, alga-coated staithe, we were welcomed into a snug outpost of civilisation with its magic window looking out on the calmness of a breathless dusk. And once we were within-doors, some of the water-birds drew near. A heron glided to a favourite fishing-stance close to the house and a pair of great crested grebes in the full splendour of their breeding plumage came close in to dive again and again in pursuit of supper. I received the impression that our lights streaming from the windows were proving a lure to shoals of fish in the broad, thus providing both grebes and heron with a special incentive to frequent the immediate vicinity of the dwelling.

A Wood in April

April 16th, 1970

Norfolk: Primroses in our eastern woods are scarcely budded and even daffodils are only just opening to this spring's reluctant sunshine. Less than a week ago I found snowdrops still glistening in a shady hollow and the scarlet-and-white cup-fungi which normally expand from rotten hazel twigs on the ground in February are only now in their full glory. The cool, dull and showery weather has favoured mosses in the countryside unaccustomed to a high rainfall at this season, so we are experiencing the unusual delight of gold-green velveting on fallen trunks and along the borders of woodland glades. With the mosses there are carpets of the translucent liverwort, *Pellia epiphylla,* now sprouting long pinhead capsules in the greatest luxuriance I have ever noted, albeit three weeks late. Sap is rising very slowly in the trees because the earth below is cold and it looks as though last year's late blossoming of hawthorns in this part of the country will be repeated. Although the leafing of hazels usually follows the dropping of catkins there is not a trace of dancing greenery on the boughs to welcome the chiffchaffs on their arrival. Lack of leafy cover has driven many a blackbird to seek nesting quarters in buildings while song thrushes attempting nidification in bushes are suffering severely from predation by jays and crows. Even the hardy honeysuckle has not yet wreathed the trees with the twining boughs beloved by early nesters. At the moment our dismal cloudland offers no prospect of comfort to the wandering cuckoo on his way.

Fog-lamp Berries

October 25th, 1974

Norfolk: Reed plumes were tossing like wave crests on an angry sea when I looked across the Yare fens today and a cold North wind was hissing through the dry and yellowing leaves. Fieldfares were coming in from the sea in scattered flocks, swooping and gliding like paper darts and appearing almost as dark as blackbirds against the heavy grey of the sky. Most of these travellers passed on, but a few were tempted to make a dive for the berries glowing like beacons on scores of guelder rose bushes, flourishing in parts of the marshland. These cousins of the common elder are really aglow at this time, not only with heavy clusters of fruits varying in colour from orange through scarlet to darkest blood red, but also foliage stained with crimson and purple. They are radiant even through the autumn mists and I have seen birds dropping out of fog and drizzle to settle and feast on them. Already the plunderers have made a start on this berry harvest and one can see red juice spattering the vegetation below, with the woody, heart-shaped pipes here and there. Recent frosts at night have hastened the colouring of leaves, while frequent showers have kept these colours fresh and sparkling. Alders have retained their funereal greenness so far, but sallows and osiers are streaked and spangled with gold. A few flowers still linger in mid-October: late bursts of meadowsweet like a froth of cream, violet blue scabious attracting a few insects in sheltered spots and even ragged robin, making its final effort to welcome the last stray butterfly which might find it during a sunny interlude.

Norfolk Reed Harvest

March 13th, 1975

Norfolk: Norfolk people take a great pride in their reeds which grow and ripen in golden profusion round the Broads. Just now, the winter harvest of the reed cutters is nearing its end. Sometimes the canes are grasped and severed with a sickle, like the corn of long ago; or, where the footing is firm, cutting is done with scythes fitted with a looped wand of hazel (called a 'bile') to clear the swathes; but on some of the larger sweeps of marshland mechanical cutters are used nowadays. Where the waters are a little brackish nearest the sea, the reeds are slender and their stems toughened by much silica; in the bays of broads enriched by nitrogenous pollution they grow tall and thick and look almost like bamboos. All types have their uses for the thatcher; he likes them short and thin for close packing, while long ones are useful for bonding and overlaps. Norfolk reed is in great demand, not only to satisfy traditional needs in East Anglia, but over a much wider field where it replaces the long thatching straw which is no longer available from farmland. When I visit friends in the Vale of Pewsey in Wiltshire I look with special pleasure at the beauty of their house, snugly thatched against a wooded hillside, because I saw those reeds growing in sturdy ranks on my own marshes, watched them being harvested the old fashioned way, stacked on the riverside, transported in flat bottomed craft to a hard staithe, hand trimmed and bunched and finally loaded almost haystack high on trucks which took them by road to Wiltshire, where local craftsmen wove them into the crowning glory of a house.

Sailing on Albion

September 5th, 1956

Brave is the breeze, alive the tide;
   Up, black sail that we may ride
From the sea's gate whither you will
   Through morning's brightness to fulful
Our dream of voyaging your way
   On such a day.

Timber and tar and salt fish reek,
   Sentinel gull and mud-flat creek,
Samphire rond, far walls of flint,
   Gloom from the clouds and the sun's glint—
Our dream of voyaging takes wings
   And the soul sings.

Redshank piper crossing our wake,
   Scarecrow cormorant on a stake,
Shelduck bobbing on the swell,
   Heron at a lonely spell—
Our dream of voyaging is bright
   As noon-day light.

Waste of waters distant now;
   Silver Yare streams by the bow;
Amethyst daisies line the shore,
   The salt tang's in the breeze no more.
Our dream of voyaging must end
   At this green bend.

*On the Wherry Albion, September 3rd, with the
Norfolk and Norwich Naturalists sailing from
Yarmouth across Breydon to Reedham.*

Scolt Head in August

Norfolk: From Brancaster Staithe, with its huddle of red and white-sailed dinghies, silver blue water merged with the sky on the western horizon and to the north, led the eye to white lines of seabirds and grass-capped dunes on Scolt Head Island. On this calm and brilliant August morning a 30-feet tide had covered the entire system of salt marshes right up to the higher pebble ridges and the parched skirts of the sandhills. Crossing to the island was like paddling within the haven of a coral-girt lagoon with a breeze so gentle that it succeeded only in dimpling the water. The bubbles riding on the slight swell came not from the foam of waves, but from little pockets of air released by flooded vegetation and its litter. Presently, stepping ashore in the farthest recess of a shallow bay, fringed with shrubby sea-blite bushes, I took a path through acres of prickly sea holly and marram grass. Thousands of grayling butterflies had been attracted by the blue flowers where they jostled endlessly with as many bumblebees, various other butterflies, small red and black moths and several recently arrived immigrant silver Y-moths. Most of these insects also flocked to the flowers of rock sea lavender at the water's edge. I found the dry places swarming with grasshoppers and a good many ladybirds, while hairy robber-flies and long-bodied sandwasps settled here and there on bare spots where the sand was almost too hot to touch in the steady blaze of the sun. I have always found the island a paradise of birds and flowers, but on this occasion it was most certainly a paradise of butterflies.

East-coast Estuary

Norfolk: The Breydon estuary, thronged with holiday craft making their way about the network of Broadland rivers in summer, looks vast and bleak at this season. Cattle grazing along its floodbanks trample the muddy turf in a way which produces strange parallel ridges, so that a walker finds the going difficult, but there are compensations in the far-flung desolation, of the marshes and the tides brimming silently over the mudflats. Stakes marking the river channel are used as perches by cormorants which stand like black gargoyles with spread wings. Small waders pass like swallows, skimming the water, or a bunch of dunlin may swirl into view and vanish like a squall of snowflakes. Gulls patrol the tideways in hungry silence. Here and there a redshank will fly up in alarm from a patch of sea-grass or a snipe will rise from a dyke and zigzag away with a brief burst of shrieking. As the tide falls, the opalescent mud becomes streaked with silver channels and herons arrive to spear smelts and flounders in the shallows. Bunches of wigeon settle on the flats where the silhouettes of curlew and oystercatcher stand sharply against the dimming light of sunset. Here and there a patch of bleached reeds fringes the high bank and in other places tidal eddies deposit white drifts of shells. Where the walls drop sheer to the water's edge they have a footing of brown bladder-wrack, then a coating of green seaweed and towards the top they are encrusted with bright orange lichen. Slithery seaslaters, like giant woodlice, lurk in the crevices and emerge with the rats to scavenge among the tide refuse

when night falls. For all its desolation, the whole of this great body of marsh and water is teeming with life, but one is hardly aware of it in the peace of an autumn afternoon.

Autumn in Broadland

November 18th, 1976

Norfolk: The vast, reedy wildernesses surrounding many of the Norfolk broads shine silver green and ripple like the sea under summer skies. The whispering of their leaves, the twittering of swallows over waters alive with bobbing waterfowl, the dark and mysterious crowding of alders and sallows in the swamps, the vivid beauty of flowers along the shore of river and lagoon: these are the delights most visitors come to know in the holiday season. Now, in autumn, the scene has changed and has a new magic. When one looks out as the bite of frost lingers in the air of a November morning and mists half veil the distances, reeds are bowed and dripping, their sodden plumes and leaves beaded with diamond points of light and the spaces between festooned with cartwheel webs of spiders. Tall willowherb

and meadow-sweet, brown, crinkled and bedraggled, stand interspersed with green spears of sedge and overhang patches of water spattered with even brighter green cresses and starwort. Dark, velvet rods of reed-mace stand in soldierly array on quaking ground, stiffly erect where all else is awry and beaten down by rain and wind. The billowy shapes of sallow bushes are spangled with autumn gold. Field-fares swoop in chattering hordes upon the crimson berries of the guelder roses in fen jungles. Shots ring out where wildfowlers are pursuing their dawn adventures and the alarms set off a flurry of nervous pheasants and screaming jays; but generally the scene is peaceful.

A Turtle's End

December 31st, 1980

Norfolk: On one of December's most wintry days I witnessed the stranding of a leatherback turtle, the second of its kind ever known to have appeared on the Norfolk coast. A monster, measuring 7ft. from nose to tail and weighing 5½ cwt., it was recognisable at once by the seven prominent ridges, like keels, running lengthwise down its dark, leathery carapace, while the immense fore-flippers lay spreadeagled and half-buried in the sand. The head had been bashed in a way which suggested impact with a ship's prow or propellor: a hazard faced by all such ocean wanderers when they stray into congested shipping lanes near our coasts. As I watched incoming breakers expend themselves in foam over this sorry carcase, with sleet sweeping upon it in icy gusts, and a leaden sky intersected by vivid rainbows forming a backcloth beyond the white water cresting the shore, I could not have imagined a more dramatic end to the saga of an ancient mariner, so far from its birthplace in the sands of some tropical beach. Considered the most primitive turtle now surviving in the world's oceans, the leatherback is the last of its line. Although, happily, it finds no favour with sea-food addicts and is not hunted, its eggs are collected as a delicacy, from the few remaining beaches where it breeds, and, were it not for vigorous efforts to protect some of the 'rookeries' from wholesale exploitation, this largest and most ancient of turtles would soon near extinction. Like the sunfishes cast away on our beaches occasionally, it is a surface-feeder, devouring salps, jellyfishes, and squids, and wandering even into Arctic waters on occasion. How it finds its way home periodically is one of the great mysteries unsolved by students of migration.

Delights of the Waveney

April 16th, 1981

Norfolk: The valley of the river Waveney, which divides Norfolk from Suffolk, is for the greater part wide and green with water meadows. The woods and thickets on its flanks harbour nightingales in summer, where sunny slopes once favoured the development of vineyards and even now are a refuge of several rare wild flowers which are absent farther north, while at its sources is a superb fen, the only remaining British haunt of the large swamp spider *(Dolomedes plantarius)*. The river itself is the least polluted of those flowing into the Broads system and in winter its upper reaches are subject to spectacular flooding whenever there are heavy rains. On the day our first swallow came home and morning mist gave way to sunshine, I went down to the Waveney at Ellingham Mill, a little below Bungay, in the knowledge that it would provide special delights in the warmth and glow of early spring at daffodil time. The white-boarded mill is now an art gallery nestling among the splendour of colourful and fragrant flower beds. Nearby, the river and adjacent mill stream tumble over a series of weirs, large and small, offering a sparkling vista of waterfalls, large and small. I found evidence of the past winter's high water levels in great wisps of flood debris caught up and held in the branches of riverside willows and other trees; but now, although the flow was still generous, there were sandy shoals and duck-haunted islands just below the influx cascading from the weirs. In this area the river was teeming with thousands of dace heading aggressively upstream. The fish were concentrated under the largest weir and many were attempting to scale the sloping concrete platforms where waters raced and foamed. They were behaving like salmon, flashing silver as they leapt and struggled forward. At times they seemed to scurry along like mice where the water was shallow in one particular place, but where a fierce, boiling current held sway, they became visible only as they darted from the foam briefly, only to be hurled back. Dace are commonly present in trout streams where there is plenty of movement in the water, but I have never before seen them leaping at waterfalls.

Old Suffolk

April 1st, 1982

Suffolk: Just south of the Waveney valley, the Suffolk countryside is rich in its diversity of meadows, treescapes, winding lanes and homesteads whose beauty has matured gently over the centuries. Here, in April, one can still find primroses, violets and cowslips flourishing by waysides and it is in this area that galaxies of snake's-head fritillaries survive in a few of the ancient cow-pastures, their future cared for by the county Trust for Nature Conservation. Being due to speak in one of the local village halls recently, I arrived on the scene in time to enjoy an evening walk by way of Brome Street to adjacent Oakley, thereby discovering all the enchantments of bygone ages woven into a tapestry of spring delights. The meanest cottage was a jewel in that patchwork of gracious trees and gardens bright with daffodils, forsythia, crocuses and snow-white arabis. Rooks were thronging tall ivied oaks and elms in whose tops they have built their nests from time immemorial and their cawing comes to the ears of all like the tolling of an evening bell, the most ancient ritual of nightfall. I glimpsed pastel pinks and golds in the limewash of masonry, half-screened by leafy shadows, with thatch and tile alternating in gentle contrast on roof-tops. At the gates of a park I came upon a rare display of artistic fantasy in brick, where stepped and moulded walls were variegated with palisades of little arches, turrets and basket patterns. There could have been no more fitting introduction to the tree-girt avenue beyond and the far-flung vista of fields and hedgerows. I saw quickthorn hedges which had been tended expertly so long that they were as compact and solid as walls. Presently I came to a roadside grove of elms in its death-throes and underneath, in a bed of glossy-leaved celandines, stood the shaggy, curry-brown remains of one of last autumn's giant puffballs. Surprisingly, while may-buds were already showing, lettuce-green, in the hedges, I found a holly still holding its full treasure of berries.

By the Water's Edge

123

March 24th, 1956

Two-year-old Susan and I took a little rug and sat down in a warm, sunny spot at the edge of a marsh dyke this morning, and we spent a happy quarter-of-an-hour just looking at the water, the dead grasses and sedges and the sheltering trees and bushes round about.

A honey bee came down to drink. A yellow brimstone butterfly came fluttering our way and little Susan suggested brightly that it was 'out of Daddy's but'fly book.' We peered into the water and could see tiny cyclops moving in jumps about green, slimy scum-weeds. A clumsy water-louse crept from under a dead leaf, reached the surface and squiggled in a leggy somersault before going down again.

There were cloudy pink patches here and there at the bottom where bacteria were swarming in places of decay. Small black-and-chestnut water beetles were scuttling about. There were floating seeds of birch, yellow flag, angelica and fluffy reed. A pretty water-fly and a springtail sported on the surface, and a pirate-spider launched itself from the edge and scurried over the water.

On the bank, we fingered pale reed leaves and examined little sooty cushions of fungus on them. Dry oak leaves blown there by the wind had spangles and pea-galls on them, and holes like pin-pricks in the pea-galls showed where the gall insects had eaten their way out. A long, narrow, pale brown plant-bug flew down on to an old reed leaf. When I lifted the leaf, it flattened itself and straightened its hind legs, pretending to be part of the reed. A robin came and sang to us and we heard red-shanks piping merrily on a meadow. Susan was very patient: we must plan more adventures like this.

Tastes in Colour

February 18th, 1978

I have found the glare of snowscapes uncomfortably dazzling in this past week, much more so than when I was younger. Young eyes are probably more swiftly accommodating than old ones when faced with bright lights. Reactions to particular colours, however, seem to vary considerably among individuals of any age. Except for those unfortunate enough to be colour-blind, most of us have the power to distinguish a wide range of hues, but it is clear that tastes are not all the same when it comes to choosing materials for a frock or the colour of a wallpaper.

There are people who take great delight in vivid colours which to others appear garish and even offensive, either singly or in juxtaposition with others. Advertisers make much use of mustard yellow and shocking 'pink', while their aggressiveness knows no bounds when neon illuminations are brought into play. Even Nature's colours can have a repellent effect. I have a vivid recollection of experiencing a feeling of sudden faintness once when I was confronted with a bowl of purplish pink tulips on opening a door from a dark passage. Occasionally I recapture childhood's glow of pleasure when I happen to catch sight of something which is a certain kind of blue or warm blue-violet, just as I, in common with a great many others, delight in crimson roses and peonies.

Similarly, particular colours come to mean more than others in the eyes of many creatures besides ourselves, especially birds and insects without whose selective influence the vast range of floral colouring would not have been evolved. Giving thought to our own reactions in a colourful scene may help us to appreciate more fully the significance of both pure and variously arranged groupings of colours in all the many niches of the living world.

Old Stone, New Stone

Cambridge, November 23rd, 1954

Old stone, new stone, and the light of spun gold on her trees,
    Her spruce-topped pinnacles, cross-figured clocks and keys;
Old stone, a sanctity of gargoyles, bluff wisdom's guys;
    New stone, young faces with the hurt of learning in their eyes.

The dappled planes are lopped in age; their pillars of bark
    A painted monument, while white wand birches rise and mark
In tenuous youth, a dayspring of new beauty by a stream
    That spills green peace where those who haunt the weeping willow dream.

All men are acolytes here, it seems: they carry books
    Like Bibles, with gentle hold and reverence in their looks.
Even as they pass on bicycles, in streaming flight
    Or stalk in duffles, gorgeous of their day, honour is bright.

Maids of Downing Street trip on their way, like sweet Jill:
    Learning for them is lavender—Cherry Ripe—what you will.
Old stone, new stone, golden leaves above a wall: I pray
To meet again the motley of these streets, so gay and grey.

The Bride

May 2nd, 1981

Early microscopes, like old cameras, have become museum pieces, but it is still fascinating to examine them as tools of pioneers who led the way to great fields of discovery in the way of aids to visual probing and recording. Rapid advances were made in the second half of the 19th century, when amateur microscopists far outnumbered the professionals.

The position has been reversed in my lifetime and we now find the most sophisticated instruments in our universities and other research centres, while most schools are furnished with equipment more serviceable than the best that were available to experts at the beginning of the century.

Nevertheless, it happens that for over 50 years I have been making regular use of a long-barrelled, narrow-staged brass microscope which first saw service in 1870.

This instrument has an interesting history. Its solid base was once a candlestick (one of a pair brought from Forder's stall in Yarmouth market place by Christopher Stacy-Watson, who fashioned the microscope to his own design). With remarkable foresight, he made the nose thread of exactly the size which was adopted universally somewhat later, so that it takes modern objective lenses.

Stacy-Watson was a keen local naturalist and published valuable papers on the herring. He lived on Yarmouth's South Quay, being a shipping agent, salt merchant and proprietor of the Yare Fishery Works until his death in 1896.

One of his close friends was Harry E. Hurrell, an ardent microscopist who in his spare time studied pond life, notably polyzoa and rotifers, on which he became expert. Stacy-Watson presented him with the candlestick microscope and he in turn gave it to me by way of encouragement for a young naturalist in my teens.

When I attended a course in marine biology at Plymouth in 1929, I took the microscope with me. Because it was draped with a silk handerchief as a dust-cover, fellow students christened it 'The Bride' and were amused by its antiquity; but it served me adequately.

I have since made thousands of drawings of fungus spores with its aid, to an accuracy of half a micro-millimetre, and the discipline of using it over the years has been of inestimable value.

It has also continued to serve as a personal link with those fellow enthusiasts with whom it was associated long ago.

Meditations

We give thanks, oh God, for the gift of Life on this earth: for all life. Thy mysteries surround us, in the depths of Space and the eternity of Time. The sunshine and the rainbow delight our eyes. In the peace of a starry night and in the shadow of the mountain we are aware of Thy presence. Our senses are comforted by the sweet distillations of flowers; our hearts are warmed by kinship with Man and Nature. Cold and heat, storm and calm, darkness and light, diversify our pilgrimage. Our spirits ebb and flow like the tides of the ocean and waves upon the shore; but to our consciousness of elemental things is added, in Mankind, a spirit of reflection and forethought, whereby we have gained stewardship of this world of ancient wealth and living wonder.

As we pause now to consider our involvement in the destiny of this glorious inheritance, let us resolve that our works henceforth may be attuned to the music that springs from our hearts in thankfulness for Thy great mercies.

In our selfishness and arrogance we have betrayed Thy trust. In our demands for luxury we have neglected the starving, wasted Thy gifts and sullied the pure air, the rivers and the seas. As we gather to ourselves the bounty of the earth, we weigh not the consequences. We isolate ourselves in pride and defiance of Thy perfect Law. We molest our fellow men and destroy the Eden of Thy creation as locusts lay waste a green land.

All of us who are gathered in this sanctuary are to some extent aware of our collective failure to honour the code of life which Thou hast set before us. We pray that we may reject what is evil and that we may discipline our actions henceforth to the furtherance of Thy design, with humility, understanding and compassion.

The above MEDITATIONS, composed by E.A. Ellis, were read in Norwich Cathedral by the Dean at a special service held during WORLD WILDLIFE YEAR.

Other titles available from
Wilson-Poole Publishers

Broadland Sketches

First published June 1979
Reprinted   June 1980
With an introductory essay by Ted Ellis

A delightful book, 80 pages of 105
illustrations and captions.
Kerrison's Level featured on the cover is
one of the drawings that capture the
unique beauty of this lovely area within
which is a surprisingly wide range of
scenic interest. A book increasingly found
to be a delightful gift for friends and
relatives.

Norfolk Coast Sketches

First published June 1980
Reprinted   May 1981
Reprinted   September 1982

A book especially appreciated for its
nostalgic content: including portraits of
fishermen and views of beautiful places
like Blakeney, Sheringham and Cromer
and including studies of King's Lynn,
Great Yarmouth and Wells. A book
particularly appreciated as a reminder to
those who love the coast's surprising
variety of feature.
Including an essay by Ted Ellis on cover.

Norwich Sketches

First published June 1981

A sketchbook of Norwich containing an
interesting mixture of pencil sketches,
drawings, watercolours and oil sketches.
96 pages of unique sketches, anecdotes
and observations of this outstandingly
lovely East Anglian city.